A Rockpool book
PO Box 252
Summer Hill
NSW 2130
Australia

rockpoolpublishing.com
Follow us! **f** [instagram icon] rockpoolpublishing
Tag your images with #rockpoolpublishing

ISBN: 9781922579256

Northern hemisphere edition
Published in 2022 by Rockpool Publishing

Design by Dana Brown, Rockpool Publishing
Typeset by Daniel Poole, Rockpool Publishing
Edited by Lisa Macken

Printed and bound in China
10 9 8 7 6 5 4 3 2 1

RECLAIMING THE MAGICK OF THE OLD WAYS

2023 WITCH'S DIARY

NORTHERN HEMISPHERE

FLAVIA KATE PETERS · BARBARA MEIKLEJOHN-FREE

ROCKPOOL

PIONEERS OF THE CRAFT

The *2023 Witch's Diary* honours all those who have given their lives to the craft. They are the founders, wisdom keepers, elders and leaders who have gone before us, who have ensured that today we hold the sacred knowledge of the ancients despite the gruesome punishments many faced and still face in mainstream society and particular cultures for their beliefs.

Let us remember those seen and unseen, known and unknown, and give our undying gratitude to all those who have shone the light of magick through the darkness.

We witches stand now side by side and strong in our beliefs while the ancestors walk beside us, and we are proud to call ourselves witches of the craft.

So mote it be.

HAIL AND WELCOME!

The *2023 Witch's Diary*, a magickal tool from which you can draw ancient wisdom, is relevant to the modern witch today and enables you to thrive in balance and harmony with a sprinkle of very real magick, in conjunction with the witches' wisdom of old.

Witches are everywhere. A witch is someone just like you who has always been drawn to nature, who naturally hears the whispers of the ancestors though the breeze, who welcomes the rains, glorifies in the heat of the sun and connects with the nourishment of the earth. A witch embraces each season and rejoices at every new bud during the first stirrings of spring, the harvest abundance that summer supplies and the falling leaves of autumn, and revels in the deep, dark mystery that accompanies the winter months.

A witch's heart sings at the mere notion of magick, has an affinity with the ways of natural healing and believes in another world of mystical beings. The natural witch is able to connect with this 'other' world,

perceiving and working in conjunction with the ancestors, whose wisdom and guidance can be drawn from: this is the way of the witch. A witch is a healer who embraces the workings of nature and takes a responsible attitude of guardianship for our beloved planet and those who reside on it.

Now more than ever you are being urged to awaken the witch within and integrate with the magick and mystery of yesteryear. As you walk along the ancient path of the witch and as an advocate of the old ways you'll find freedom to express who you truly are and reclaim your personal power as you harness the magick of nature and the innate powers of witches' wisdom.

The *2023 Witch's Diary* is ideal for any nature lover who wishes to bring the magick of the old ways into their everyday lives. Each month you'll discover how to work with specific moon phases and weekdays in order to harness your personal power and enhance your magickal abilities. Journey through the year as you work with the forces of nature through spell work, incantations, recipes, herbs and much more.

This diary is perfect for both the seasoned witch and those who are exploring the ancient path of the wise. Each page is a magical avenue to draw upon ancient wisdom that is still relevant for the modern witch today.

You'll find each page assists you well
Through incantation, message, spell.
Tools explained, history unearthed
Allowing magick to be birthed.
The witch in you will be empowered
No more will others leave you soured.
Look no further than inside:
It's here the magick doth reside.

Blessed be,
Flavia and Barbara

MOON PHASES

The moon has always fascinated humankind, its luminosity hinting at our celestial origins, and it's no wonder the ancients worshipped it as the goddess herself. All things in life are interconnected, so the frequencies emanating from the moon can affect your feelings and emotions. When you become acquainted with the moon's phases you'll know when to cast certain spells and when to access its energies for its particular transformational powers.

~ Dark or old moon ~

This phase is a powerful time to remove and banish things, people or situations, a time to neutralise spells made against others. It is also a potent time for understanding your fears and anger and for bringing about justice.

Time of transition from a dark moon to a new moon.

~ Waxing crescent moon ~

This phase is for constructive magick to increase things, for fresh beginnings and relationships and for sowing seeds for new ventures. It is the best time to focus on and set your intentions for positive outcomes.

~ First quarter moon ~

This phase is the optimum time to draw things in such as money, success, friends, lovers and work, and for attracting what you most desire into manifestation. It also indicates a period of acceleration and growth.

~ Waxing gibbous moon ~

This phase is about the renewal of strength and energy. It is a time to focus on willpower and seeing things through and to surrender to the universe and trust. This is the most powerful moon phase for fruition and completion.

~ Full moon ~

During a full moon what no longer serves you will be released and you can harness extra power to overcome difficult challenges. This is a time of manifestation when you can use rituals and spells for protection and divination and for healing long-standing illnesses. A full moon is the most powerful one and its magick is potent.

~ Waning gibbous moon ~

This is a great time to expel all negative thoughts and influences. Waning moon energies rid and repel, so it is a time to decrease, to bring things to an end, and a time of facing your shadows.

~ Last quarter moon ~

This is a phase of transitions, and for removing obstacles and avoiding temptations.

~ Waning crescent moon ~

With this phase comes a transition between the death of the old and the birth of the new. It is a time of banishment and retreat.

Between a dark moon and a waxing crescent moon is a period of stillness called a new moon, which is the space between the past and new beginnings. This is a very powerful phase of transition.

LUNAR AND SOLAR ECLIPSES

Eclipses are magickal astrological events that can fuel a witch's intentions, wishes and spells with cosmic energy to manifest new beginnings and empowering, positive change.

Solar eclipses occur during a new moon. When the sun, moon and earth are in alignment the moon casts a shadow across the earth that fully or partially blocks out the sun. For witches, a solar eclipse means truly transforming and harnessing the magick of fresh beginnings.

Lunar eclipses occur only during a full moon. When the sun and earth are in close alignment the moon moves into the earth's shadow and becomes fully or partially obscured. For witches, a lunar eclipse means harnessing the magick of empowerment and manifestation.

2023

20 April: partial solar eclipse.

5-6 May: penumbral lunar eclipse.

14 October: annular solar eclipse (ring of fire).

28-29 October: partial lunar eclipse.

2024

24-25 March: penumbral lunar eclipse.

8 April: total solar eclipse.

17-18 September: partial lunar eclipse.

2 October: annular solar eclipse.

17 October: almost total lunar eclipse.

FULL MOONS

A full moon usually happens once a month; when there are two full moons in a month it's called a blue moon. The phase of a full moon is when magick for manifesting is at its optimum. Each full moon has a variety of names relating to the month and a unique mystical energy that can be harnessed to enhance your own magickal workings.

JANUARY: olde, frost, birch, cold moon.
Letting go of the past and invoking the new.

FEBRUARY: ice, snow, rowen, quickening.
The journey of the soul inwards.

MARCH: moon of winds, storm, ash, worm, crow.
Coming from the darkness to the light.

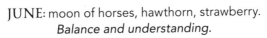

APRIL: growing, alder, seed.
Growth and the planting of new ideas.

MAY: hare, milk, bright, willow.
Attention to your needs and of those you love.

JUNE: moon of horses, hawthorn, strawberry.
Balance and understanding.

JULY: hay, thunder, mead, oak.
Making plans for the future.

AUGUST: corn, holly, grain.
Removing excess baggage and being flexible.

SEPTEMBER: harvest, hazel, fruit, barley.
Completion and future prospects.

OCTOBER: blood, vine, hunter's moon.
Soul growth and deep inner wisdom.

NOVEMBER: snow, ivy, dark.
Truth and honesty and reassessing your life.

DECEMBER: wolf, elder, cold.
The healing of old wounds and emotions.

THE WHEEL OF THE YEAR

Spiritual wisdom can be gained by recognising the traditions of old witchcraft and the connection to the seasons. As the witches of old worked with the elemental forces of nature, they also honoured the aspects of the triple goddess in relation to the seasons and festivals celebrated through the wheel of the year.

In nature the year is made up of four seasons. The sun marks any seasonal change, and these changes are honoured by celebrating four solar festivals. Fire festivals are marked by cross-quarter and equinox celebrations, so altogether eight festivals of the seasons become the wheel of the year. These festivals represent the state of nature at the time, the agricultural calendar and the physical and spiritual effects the time of year has on humankind.

From planting in spring to harvesting in autumn, the seasons are of great importance. Different celebrations mark times to count our blessings, for reaping and recognising all that we've sowed and for giving thanks to the nature spirits and to the goddess in her triple aspect of maiden, mother and crone as she continues the circle that we call life on earth.

CROSS-QUARTER FESTIVALS AND EQUINOXES

IMBOLC, 1 February: this is a time of fresh growth, as new shoots appear from the ground and we begin to witness the start of the renewal of life. The maiden: innocence, purity, seeding the dream and birthing the inner child.

OSTARA, 19-22 March: this is a time when balance hangs in the air and the length of the day equals that of the night, and we celebrate the birth of new life. The maiden matures: from dark to light we explore signs of growth and discernment.

BELTANE, 1 May: this fire festival celebrates the full bloom of nature. The mother: fertile minds, bodies and souls, birthing our ideas and the soul's knowing.

LITHA, 19-22 June: this festival celebrates the summer solstice, the longest day of the year. The mother glorified: a celebration of light and being in our full glory.

LUGHNASADH, 1 August: the time when the grain harvest is cut down and celebrated. The mother matures: gratitude for earthly, physical sustenance.

MABON, 21-24 September: during this time day and night are balanced and the fruit harvest is celebrated. The crone: the art of contemplation is explored and there is self-sufficiency of mind, body and spirit.

SAMHAIN, 31 October: a time to honour the souls of the dead and when the veil between the worlds is at its thinnest. The crone revered: respecting our ancestors and healing our hurts.

YULE, 20-23 December: the winter solstice is a celebration of the rebirth of the sun, for now that the longest night has arrived the nights thereafter will start to grow shorter. The crone fades: the returning of the sun and an exploration of the purest energy that is the essence of our being.

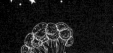

PLANTING AND HARVESTING DAYS

Witches have always planted according to the moon cycles and in conjunction with the movement of the planets, because they understand that different plants grow better when they are planted during different phases of the moon. Each of these phases influences the way vegetation grows through the rising and falling of the moisture in the ground and in the plants, but it's not just planting that is the most important time for the farmer as harvest time also has to be considered. Harvesting at the correct time ensures crops last much longer: it is down to how the plants store water at different times of the moon cycle.

NEW MOON: an excellent time to sow leafy plants such as cabbages, broccoli, celery and cauliflower and to transplant leafy annuals.

WAXING MOON: sap flows and rises, so this is a good time for new growth. Sow or transplant flowering annuals, biennials and grains and plant fruits or flowers that are to be harvested.

FIRST QUARTER MOON: this is the time to plant tomatoes, beets, broccoli, beans and squashes.

FULL MOON: during a full moon sow or plant root crops such as potatoes and asparagus and fruit perennials such as apples and rhubarb. It is the perfect time for separating plants and taking cuttings.

WANING MOON: sap is drawn down during a waning moon, so plant perennials and root crops. It is a good time to prune and harvest.

LAST QUARTER MOON: this is the time to weed, dig or plough and to improve the soil with compost or manure.

PLANET RULERS AND SIGNS

Each zodiac sign is affiliated with a planet that is said to be its ruler. The ruling planet adds a dimension to the sign it rules and influences how the sign is expressed, giving insights into the personality traits intrinsic within the sign.

 ARIES
Mars

 TAURUS
Venus

 GEMINI
Mercury

 CANCER
The moon

 LEO
The sun

 VIRGO
Mercury

 LIBRA
Venus

 SCORPIO
Mars

 SAGITTARIUS
Jupiter

 CAPRICORN
Saturn

 AQUARIUS
Uranus

 PISCES
Neptune

THE GODDESS AND MOON PHASES

The goddess is worshipped in conjunction with the phases of the moon – waxing, full and waning – which represent the three phases of the goddess as maiden, mother and crone.

~ MAIDEN ~

ASPECTS: beauty, enchantment, inception, expansion, new beginnings, youth, excitement, virginity, innocence.

Season: spring.

Colour: white.

Moon phase: waxing.

Festivals: Imbolc, Ostara (spring equinox).

~ MOTHER ~

ASPECTS: ripeness, fertility, growth, fulfilment, stability, giving, nurturing, compassion.

Season: summer.

Colour: red.

Moon phase: full.

Festivals: Beltane, Litha (summer solstice), Lughnasadh.

~ CRONE ~

ASPECTS: wisdom, repose, magick, destruction, decay, death.

Season: winter.

Colour: black.

Moon phases: waning, dark, new.

Festivals: Mabon (autumn equinox), Samhain (Hallowe'en), Yule (winter solstice).

MAGICKAL WEEKDAYS

Witches adhere to specific magickal timings such as weekdays to enhance their magickal practice and work with universal energies while they are at their most potent in relation to the chosen spell.

~ SUNDAY ~

The day of the god Apollo, ruled by the sun: this day is imbued with energy and divine guidance and is perfect for relaxing, unwinding and focusing on health and well-being to light up your inner sunshine.

~ MONDAY ~

The day of the goddess Diana, ruled by the moon: this is a day for discovering your true potential and intuition and for looking deep within and honouring your emotions.

~ TUESDAY ~

The day of Týr, ruled by Mars: a day for projects, decision making and new jobs and to take steps to fulfil your dreams, goals and desires.

~ WEDNESDAY ~

The day of the god Woden (Odin), ruled by Mercury: a day to express yourself and focus on life decisions and for communication and messages.

~ THURSDAY ~

The day of the god Thor, ruled by Jupiter: a day of gratitude and positivity and a time of expansion of your mind, body and spirit.

~ FRIDAY ~

The day of the goddess Frigg, ruled by Venus: a day of love and self-care and a time to create and connect with others.

~ SATURDAY ~

The day of the god Saturn: a great day to tackle big projects and be responsible and get organised both at home and at work. It is also a time to be grounded and balanced.

MAGICKAL MOON TIMES
TO CAST SPELLS

~ DARK MOON ~
from dawn to sunset.

~ WAXING CRESCENT MOON ~
from mid-morning to after sunset.

~ FIRST QUARTER MOON ~
from noon until midnight.

~ WAXING GIBBOUS MOON ~
from mid-afternoon until 3 am.

~ FULL MOON ~
from sunset to dawn.

~ WANING GIBBOUS MOON ~
from mid-evening until mid-morning.

~ LAST QUARTER MOON ~
from midnight until noon.

~ WANING CRESCENT MOON ~
from 3 am until mid-afternoon.

MAGICKAL MEANINGS OF COLOURS

Colour is a natural source of cosmic energy that a witch can draw upon. Every colour has its own vibration and its own unique resonance that can be harnessed for magickal spells and healing and used in the form of, for example, coloured candles, cloth or crystals.

~ WHITE ~
purification, blessings, aspect of light, cosmos.

~ BLACK ~
elimination, banishment, retribution, north, earth.

~ BLUE ~
peace, harmony, healing, curing fevers, re-igniting friendships, house blessings.

~ BROWN ~
grounding, stabilising, intuition, balance, connection to Mother Earth.

~ GOLD ~
cosmic influences, solar deities, success, wealth, influence.

~ GREEN ~
fertility, good fortune, generosity, wealth, success, renewal, marriage, healing.

~ INDIGO ~
meditation, balancing karma, stopping gossip, astral projection.

~ MAGENTA ~
rapid change, spiritual healing, exorcism.

~ ORANGE ~
communication, telepathy, new job, adaptability, luck, control, attraction.

~ PINK ~
romance, affection, love, spiritual awakening, unity.

~ PURPLE ~
honour, respect, wisdom, divine knowing, trust, spiritual connection.

~ SILVER ~
moon magick, protection from entities, inner peace, serenity.

Magickal directions and elements

Each direction is assigned to one of the four basic elements of earth, air, fire and water; without them this planet would be lifeless. The four basic elements work in harmony with each other and with the fifth element of spirit, which runs through everything to create and sustain life. Each of the four basic elements is associated with a direction, a season and a moon phase when it comes to magickal workings, and we acknowledge above, below and within. Witches work naturally with the forces of nature and call upon the guardians of each direction when creating sacred space and before ritual and spell casting.

~ NORTH ~
the element of earth and the season of winter;
a time of the new moon and midnight.

~ WEST ~
the element of water and the season of autumn; *a time of the waning moon and dusk.*

~ EAST ~
the element of air and the season of spring; *a time of the waxing moon and sunrise.*

~ SOUTH ~
the element of fire and the season of summer;
a time of the full moon and noon.

~ ABOVE ~
mind connection with the universal great mystery.

~ BELOW ~
body connection with the earth.

~ WITHIN ~
spirit connection with your inner universe, the great void.

TREES OF POWER

Ancient and enduring and known as the standing ones, trees are wisdom keepers and mystical gateways to the otherworld. Trees have long been associated with witches, for they hold the magical secrets of yesteryear and are extreme sources of power upon a witch can draw. The spirits of the trees are multidimensional and they each have their own magickal properties.

ALDER: resurrection, rebirth, fire.

APPLE: healing, prosperity, love, peace, happiness, youth.

ASH: healing, protection, sea magick.

BIRCH: new beginnings and births, fertility, purifications, protection, blessings.

BLACKTHORN: bad luck, strife, unexpected changes, death, wounding, curses.

CEDAR: purification, prosperity, longevity; represents the earth and spirituality.

ELDER: healing, love, protection, prosperity; used to make magickal wands.

ELM: primordial female powers, protection.

FIR: youth, vitality; used in prosperity magick.

HAWTHORN: female sexuality, cleansing, marriage, love, protection; a magickal tool.

HAZEL: fertility, divination, marriage, protection, reconciliation; used to make wands.

HOLLY: protection.

OAK: healing, strength, longevity.

PINE: immortality, fertility, health, prosperity; represents the earth.

ROWAN: protection, healing, strength; represents fire.

WILLOW: moon and wishing magick, healing, protection, enchantments; represents water.

YEW: immortality, rebirth, protection, longevity, change, divinity, strength.

TREE INCANTATION

Time to seek trees for the wisdom they weave
Magick is found if you truly believe.
So feel the pull of old sacred land
Drawing you in to where ancient trees stand.
Energy potent, feeling the flow
Magickally charged now and ready to go!

2023 WITCH'S DIARY

MONTHS

JANUARY

Olde, frost, birch, cold moon

Letting go of the past, invoking the new.

January brings the energy of a new start as the calendar year begins. In the northern hemisphere the cold, hard earth remains steeped in deep magick and mystery, nurturing and restoring all that resides within it and offering comfort from the hardships and discomfort that the glacial callousness of winter brings. The goddess is in her crone phase, but now she is beginning to fade as the promise of new life beckons and the days are getting longer since her deathly reign of winter and the solstice at Yule. This is a time of slow awakening for all of nature and to look at fresh goals as you leave old regrets behind and make new resolutions through intention, ritual and spells to assist you through the months of the long year that awaits.

It is time to take the first brave steps of authenticity towards the magickal freedom of embracing the witch within, to stop hesitating and hiding in the shadows. Bid farewell to negativity, control and disempowerment and embrace the lessons of the past as the door closes on yesteryear and brighter experiences await. The crone offers you rebirth and transformation as you follow the wheel of the year and the magick of the old ways.

GODDESS: **Danu (Celtic/Irish)**, first great mother, earth goddess, cosmic triple goddess.

CRONE: transformation, dreams, clarity, wisdom, alchemical magick.

MOON MAGICK

Your fate is sealed when the moon goddess Arianrhod spins her silver wheel and, just like the dead souls who wait for her to decide on their kismet before facing reincarnation, you would be wise not to avoid her. Be watchful of cyclical emotions that could overwhelm and deter you from the path you seek. Instead, even though her purposeful life lessons might leave you blinded in the darkness of despair for a while, you must trust in the deep wisdom of the deaths and endings that have gone before. What is written in the stars for you awaits, and the brightness of Arianrhod's silver wheel beckons the light of your inner knowing now her lessons have been embraced. It is she who shines moonlight upon your path of destiny, to show you the way now woven towards a brighter future and the year ahead.

MOON: DESTINY

A path that glitters is revealed
Follow, for your fate is sealed.
Seek, unlock the truth this night
And walk towards the shining light.

26 Monday

27 Tuesday

28 Wednesday

29 Thursday

30 Friday

First quarter moon · Maxine Sanders (1946-), high priestess and occultist.

31 Saturday

1 Sunday

Over 40,000 to 50,000 executions occurred in witch-hunts between 1450 and 1750; this does not include witch-hunts that were not recorded.

NEW YEAR SPELL

When a full moon hangs in the sky, embrace its power as you draw down its magick and mystery and the embodiment of the goddess, for she is the vessel from which all things spring forth. Feel the power of the goddess surging through you, allowing her to move and work through you as you accept her gift of empowerment. Soon you will have control over your life and the confidence to support others while standing in your power.

Stand under the moon, hold a moonstone crystal in your left hand and with your arms outstretched say:

On this bright night, I draw down the moon
Oh goddess, speak through me; empower me soon.
Fears to face first, a journey within
Power reclaimed, let the ritual begin.
New year ahead, I won't look back
Power of moon sets me back on track.
Gratitude for all lessons learned
Destiny calls, future discerned.
Moonstone now placed upon third eye
Fuelling new strength for visions to scry.
The witch within now birthed to embrace
Magick now claimed, four seasons to face.
I draw down the moon and welcome the year
And stand in my power with nothing to fear.

Bury the moonstone in the earth under the light of the moon to restore, recharge and reclaim your magick as a witch.

WITCHY TIP

Create a moon altar with a silver cloth, a small wheel or crystal sphere, two silver candles and moonstone crystals. Under a full moon, weave silver thread around your left wrist as you focus on your destiny and say: *'I am a weaver of my fate. I am now woven into my destiny.'*

KITCHEN WISDOM

TURMERIC: I'm here to make a difference in your magickal pantry, for a little diversity is needed to shake things up. Old routines have become stale and your magick a little worn. It's time to add variation to the mundane and take a leaf out of my book, for my natural powers go beyond the ordinary as any hedge witch will confirm. My strong anti-inflammatory properties are used to treat a variety of ailments; from increasing antioxidant capacity to helping fight free radical damage, I help boost the immune system and protect the heart and have even been known to lift your mood. I can also add an element of deliciousness to food when you stir in my yellow powder, particularly curry, and I contribute to healthy digestion. My magickal powers can be utilised to remove black magick and curses will lift when you use my black powder, which is not for consumption! Opportunities for change and a new outlook arise as the year begins and I remind you that variety really is the spice of life.

2 Monday

3 Tuesday

4 Wednesday
Doreen Valiente (1922-99), mother of modern witchcraft, United Kingdom.

5 Thursday
Barbara Meiklejohn-Free (1957-), high priestess, highland seer and occultist, United Kingdom.

6 Friday
Full moon.

7 Saturday

8 Sunday
Samuel Liddell MacGregor Mathers (1854-1918), one of the founders of the Hermetic Order of the Golden Dawn, London, United Kingdom.

9   Monday

....

10   Tuesday

....

11   Wednesday
The trial of the Basque witches began in January 1609 in Logroño, Spain.

....

12   Thursday

....

13   Friday

....

14   Saturday

....

15   Sunday
Third quarter moon.

WITCHY RECIPE

This golden smoothie is great for acid reflux and hypothyroidism. Throw into your blender 3 teaspoons of turmeric, 1 teaspoon of ginger powder, 1 teaspoon of cinnamon powder, 2 bananas, 10 fresh basil leaves, 2 tablespoons of aloe vera gel and 2 cups of milk. Mix well and taste, and add honey for sweetening. Make a batch to keep in the fridge and drink it first thing in the morning.

TURMERIC: DIVERSITY

Routine's old and very stale
Mundane tasks lead you to fail.
Mix me in to welcome change
Diversity reveals new range.
This magick is worked, with harm to none.
So mote it be; there, it is done.

16   Monday

17   Tuesday

18   Wednesday

19   Thursday

In Valais, Switzerland 367 people were condemned for witchcraft from 1428 to 1448.

20   Friday

21   Saturday

New moon.

22   Sunday

In Trier, Germany 368 people were condemned for witchcraft from 1581 to 1593.

23 Monday

24 Tuesday
Theoris of Lemnos (fourth century BCE), Greek witch folk healer, executed.

25 Wednesday

26 Thursday

27 Friday

28 Saturday
First quarter moon · Agnes Sampson burned as a witch in 1591 in the Royal Mile, Edinburgh.

29 Sunday

FEBRUARY

Ice, snow, rowen, quickening moon

—◇—

A time of purification and hope.

After the harshness of winter this is a time of emergence as new shoots appear from the ground, early flowers begin to blossom and we begin to witness the start of the renewal of life. Daylight hours finally start to become noticeably longer at this time and we celebrate the birth of the very first lambs as the ewes start to lactate. It was an important time for our ancestors as fresh milk once again became available, meaning the difference between life and death after the cold, harsh scarcity of winter.

—◇—

IMBOLC: 1 February

—◇—

GODDESS: **Bridget (Celtic/Irish)**, new life, hope, growth.

MAIDEN: innocence, purity, seeding the dream.

~ Imbolc ~

First signs of new growth

Today at Imbolc it is still tradition to pour fresh milk on the ground to honour Mother Earth and to ensure fertility for the coming season. In agriculture, this is when seeds are planted and we see signs of flowers such as snowdrops and crocuses starting to grow.

Imbolc is a time of purification in preparation for the coming year and is portrayed by the virginal maiden aspect of the Celtic triple goddess. She is the young girl awakening to womanhood just as nature begins its fertility cycle and offers us new life and new beginnings. This is the time to seed your new ideas, to make plans and begin creative projects that will grow into fruition through the coming warmer months. As nature starts to wake up it is a time to awaken and create fresh dreams and goals.

IMBOLC INCANTATION

'Neath a layer of soft white snow
Doth a single flower grow.
The goddess stands in maiden form
Shining through this very dawn.
New fruits stir her virgin womb
Awakening from winter's tomb.
She calls to you to be free
Explore each possibility.
For now is when to seed your dreams
No matter how hard and tough life seems.
They will come true; it's time to trust
Be one with nature, don't fight or thrust.
Take the cup she offers you
That's filled with milk from a ewe.
Embrace the year through open eyes
Magick awaits, nature tells no lies.

30 Monday

The persecution of witches in Rome continued until the late fourth century CE.

31 Tuesday

1 Wednesday

Imbolc, Candlemas.

2 Thursday

3 Friday

4 Saturday

5 Sunday

Full moon · Janet Horne was the last woman in the United Kingdom to be legally executed for witchcraft, in 1727.

WITCH'S WISDOM

To understand the regenerative cycles of nature, witches pursue opportunities for growth, change and new beginnings. With a dark journey at its end the transformation your soul craves has already started to birth, for it was your deep, silent wishes and desires to magickally evolve, to live as your authentic self, that invited in a process of awakening in order to tear through the veil of illusion. You must prepare to replace illusions of the past while a much more ancient wisdom and magick seeks you out. Light cutting through the darkness reveals the path of ultimate spiritual transformation and growth that you are to take. The midwife within offers her nurturing, supporting care as you travel through the birth canal of the unknown and towards the promise of new life to embrace your soul's awakening.

INCANTATION

Awaken now from barren tomb
As fertile fruits stir virgin womb.
Through the darkness new light gleams
Birthing hope to seed the dream.
This magick is worked with harm to none.
So mote it be; there, it is done.

WITCHY TIP

Fertility rites and initiation into becoming a woman were common practice for our witchy ancestors. Midwives supported one another and recognised the grail goddess within. The grail represented a cauldron, which symbolises the power of creation within the womb and represents the womb of the goddess, in turn a symbol of the dark void before creation in which all life begins. The cauldron contains the potential of all creation and all primordial forces, and when its contents are stirred up it contains a recipe for magick. The womb space you carry is an energetic vortex with the power to create new life.

6   Monday

....

7   Tuesday

Persecution of the Cathars in France around 1450 for witchcraft and heresy.

....

8   Wednesday

Éliphas Lévi Zahed, greatest occultist of the 19th century.

....

9   Thursday

....

10   Friday

....

11   Saturday

....

12   Sunday

13 Monday
Third quarter moon.

14 Tuesday

15 Wednesday

16 Thursday
Pamela Colman Smith (1878–1951), occultist, artist of the Rider-Waite tarot.

17 Friday

18 Saturday

19 Sunday
Over 5,000 members of the Bacchus cult were executed between 182 and 184 BCE by the Roman senate for practising witchcraft at the ecstatic rites of Dionysus.

KITCHEN WITCHERY

THYME: resistance is futile as you walk the witch's solitary path of no return, for once magick is born within it can never die. I will support you as you step out of the witchy broom closet and declare to the world who you really are. It's time to burn brightly as you resolve to commit to your magickal path no matter what the opinions of others are. Know that you are safe as you massage in my oil, as the warriors of old did, to induce the courage needed for battle. As you face challenges head on I will reinforce your bravery and strength.

Add thyme to your bath water or sew it into your undergarments to increase vigour, and weave it into your hair to enhance allurement.

WITCHY RECIPE

This vapour rub will clear sinuses, colds and chest infections. Using a double boiler, bring water to the boil and simmer. Add to the inner pan 40 grams of olive oil, 1.5 grams of menthol crystals and 7.5 grams of beeswax. Once the mixture has melted, take the pan off the heat and allow it to cool. Add in a few drops of thyme essential oil along with nutmeg, eucalyptus and sage. Pour into a jar or tin and allow to set before using.

NEW CAREER SPELL

Take three ribbons and plait them together as you
focus on your desired career, then say:

Stagnant, dreary, job's a bore
Focus, change, cannot ignore.
Intentions weaved, make them my goal
Invent, embrace the perfect role.
Time to soar, eager to fly
The only way is up; aim high.
Ladder of success I'll climb
Dream job offered; finally mine.

Pin the braid of ribbons as high up as you can to a tree,
ladder or wall to fly high in your chosen career.

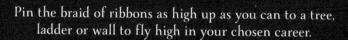

20 Monday
New moon.

21 Tuesday

22 Wednesday
La Voisin (1640–80), French fortune teller, sorceress and commissioned poisoner; burned at the stake · Sybil Leek (1917–82), witch, occult author and astrologer.

23 Thursday

24 Friday

25 Saturday
Forty-five men and 85 women suspected of sorcery were executed in the reign of Tibetus Claudius, from 41 to 54 CE.

26 Sunday

MARCH

Moon of winds, storm, ash, worm, crow moon

Coming from the darkness growing into the light.

In like a lion and out like a lamb, the winds of change welcome in this wild month, which brings hope of warmer days to come. The energy at this waxing time of year becomes expansive as the light grows strong enough to defeat the dark, and the natural world comes alive as the sun gains strength and brings the promise of longer and warmer days. As the goddess in her maiden form walks across the land breathing new life into the world, all of nature wakes up to the fulfilled promises made at Imbolc. Spring has sprung!

OSTARA: 19-22 March

GODDESS: Eostre/Ostara (Anglo/Germanic), spring, fertility, renewal, fruitfulness.

MAIDEN: the dark of the old aligns with new light, signs of growth and creative power.

~ OSTARA ~

Alignment of the natural world

Ostara heralds the spring equinox, a time of balance between light and dark and a day of equilibrium. When you are aligned with the natural world you can embrace and honour the new creative power that is stirring throughout nature.

Ostara is a time for honouring new life and is the festival that was borrowed from age-old traditions to become Easter: think hatched eggs, baby chicks, moon-gazing hares and all the fresh promises of spring. Call upon the spirits of the air to enhance your creativity and meditation abilities and to stimulate your mind as you light incense and a yellow candle and face the direction of east. This is a great time for fertility as air blows you in the direction of new beginnings, so throw caution to the wind and watch as your visions manifest into reality.

OSTARA INCANTATION

Celebrate the stirring of spring
Natural balance, doth it bring.
Claim that of which it represents;
New life, growth and expectance.
Seeds planted in nature's tomb
Incubate within her womb.
Symbolic hares upon the lawn
Herald the goddess of the dawn.
And from the east the sun doth rise
Shining bright across the skies.
The goddess works behind the scenes
To manifest your goals and dreams.
Await and trust now; it is the key.
For life will bloom most readily.

27 Monday

First quarter moon · Comte de Saint Germain (1712–84), Hungarian alchemist and philosopher.

28 Tuesday

1 Wednesday

First Witchcraft Act in England in 1542; the instigator was Henry VIII.

2 Thursday

3 Friday

4 Saturday

5 Sunday

WITCH'S WISDOM

There's not a gardener in the world who worships and understands nature quite like a witch does, for the path of the green witch is tied to ancient tradition and ritual, the roots of which were forged centuries ago with the ancestors of old. Now is the time to get your hands dirty, to dig deep within and unearth your natural affinity with the world of flora and fauna. As you sow, plant and tend your own plot think outside the window box for a moment and listen for the subtle messages of wisdom emitting from the plant world. Each variety has its own restorative properties and unique healing ability that you can draw and learn from. You never need to stray far from the garden gate, for a herb garden of your very own will supply you with the pick of the crop when it comes to choosing cures for ailments and growing ingredients for magickal recipes in your own backyard.

INCANTATION

Secret gardens of medicinal powers
Magick hidden in plants, herbs and flowers.
Mystical cures to bring about ease
From soothing the skin, to healing disease.
This magick is worked with harm to none.
So mote it be; there, it is done.

WITCHERY

If you don't have a space for a garden, grow a few magickal herbs in a window box for spells, healing and charms:

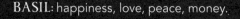

BASIL: happiness, love, peace, money.

MINT: banishment.

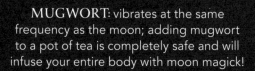

MUGWORT: vibrates at the same frequency as the moon; adding mugwort to a pot of tea is completely safe and will infuse your entire body with moon magick!

ROSEMARY: psychic protection, peace of mind, prevents nightmares.

SAGE: cleansing, purification.

THYME: courage, strength, positive attitude.

MOON-GAZING HARE
INCANTATION

Allure of the moon, hypnotic haze
Bewitching trance as he looks up to gaze.
Mad as March and quick as a flash
Bewitching illusion compelled now to dash.
This moon magick is said and done.
So mote it be, with harm to none.

6 Monday
Laurie Cabot (1933-), high priestess and occultist, Salem, United States.

7 Tuesday
Full moon.

8 Wednesday

9 Thursday
Between the 4th and 6th centuries CE more than 1,000 witches were persecuted and expelled from the Huns, a nomadic tribe.

10 Friday

11 Saturday

12 Sunday
Hypatia (360–415 CE), ancient philosopher, astronomer; murdered by a mob who accused her of witchcraft.

13 Monday

14 Tuesday

15 Wednesday
Third quarter moon.

16 Thursday

17 Friday

18 Saturday
Manly Palmer Hall (1901-90), mystic and astrologer.

19 Sunday

KITCHEN WITCHERY

ST JOHN'S WORT: when your hope has been shattered and you're feeling downright miserable, reach for my bright yellow flowers to restore your former sunny disposition. The effectiveness of my antidepressant properties will cheer you up in no time, and soon your natural sparkle will return to you in full. As I spirit away any feelings of guilt and poor self-worth, take care not to tread on me or a faery horse may steal you away! Drink me as a tea to soothe rheumatism, neuralgia and the symptoms of menopause, or place me in the garden and I'll attract bees to colour up your life as you begin to blossom again.

WITCHY RECIPE

This salve is great for tired muscles and back pain. Put 60 grams of St John's wort–infused oil, 45 grams of dandelion-infused oil, 18 grams of beeswax and a few drops of vitamin E in a double boiler. Place over low heat until the wax melts. Take off the heat, cool and add in your favourite essential oil. Pour into a tin and store in a cool place.

WITCH'S FAMILIAR

WREN: stop blocking out my cheerful song! When your chatty mind works overtime it dulls your senses. My mission is to raise your awareness so you can observe your own perceptions and understand the apprehensions of others. You are bold, and as a free spirit you need to live your life in a carefree way. It's time to fly out of your comfort zone, to be alert to messages from spirit and to inspire others. Be the mesmeriser: draw others in to open their minds to different possibilities and bridge the gap between the material and spiritual worlds. It is time to branch out and change direction and follow the winds of self-realisation that beckon you into new awareness.

WREN: AWARENESS

Awaken one and all this morn
To tuneful songs upon the dawn.
Observe to grasp and understand
Awareness raised across the land.
I call upon wren to assist me
And harness this power. So mote it be.

20 Monday
Ostara, spring equinox.

21 Tuesday
New moon.

22 Wednesday

23 Thursday

24 Friday

25 Saturday

26 Sunday
Zhang Liang executed for treason and witchcraft in 646 CE.

27 Monday

28 Tuesday

29 Wednesday
First quarter moon · Granny Boswell (1813–1909), well-known local witch in Cornwall; married the king of the witches.

30 Thursday

33 Friday

1 Saturday
Second Witchcraft Act in England in 1563; the instigator was Elizabeth I.

2 Sunday

FERTILITY SPELL

At sunrise, face the direction of east, hold an egg in your hand
and infuse it with your wishes and new ideas. Say:

Upon the dawn, stand facing east
Egg in hand for Ostara feast.
Ideas conceived, won't be long
Goals and wishes, growing strong.
Plant the egg into the earth
Fertile land assists this birth.
Creative fuel, inspired and known
New life poised to claim and own.

Make a nest for the egg or bury it in the earth to incubate, so that
your goals and ideas can grow into fruition over the coming months.

APRIL

Growing, alder, seed moon

Growth, planting and connecting with the magick of nature.

The fresh light rain of April brings with it fresh ideas and inspiration. This is a great time for wishes and magick as the earth springs forth and faeries tend to and nurture their wards, the newly growing flowers. For thousands of years witches and healers have worked alongside the power of the fae, who have shared ancient knowledge of healing herbs, cures and ointments with those who have visited their mystical world. A new magickal energy of growth surrounds you and the faeries are poised to support you as any heartfelt wishes reflect your thoughts and good intentions. They are the guardians of nature who remind you that magick is everywhere and in everything, so go outside and discover it! Enjoy every precious moment, knowing and appreciating that you are totally blessed as you feel the faery witch within stir deeply.

GODDESS: **Cordelia (Celtic/British)**, faery queen of flowers, faeries, beauty and wishes.

MAIDEN: renewing the spirit and inhaling fresh air and the fragrance of spring flowers.

WITCH'S WISDOM

An affinity with the ways of natural healing and a belief in another world of mystical beings make your heart sing at the mere notion of elemental magick. Step into the world of the fae, a shining world within our own of elemental guardians who preside over the elements of earth, air, fire and water to support the ways of nature through their natural workings of miracles and magick. The faeries are waiting and are present in every flower, leaf, rock and stone. Will you not acknowledge them and take a step sideways to become part of their magick to ensure the natural balance in all things? A witch keeps a foot in both worlds and has sought out faery folk through the ages for their knowledge of earth magick. As you become more open to the natural world of elemental magick it will seek you out: ancient pathways will show themselves, hidden doorways will be revealed and other portals will open to you, enhancing your natural magick and giving you entry to the faery realm.

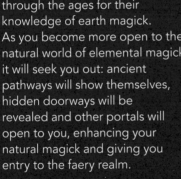

INCANTATION

The magick of earth manifests my desire
Embrace now the power of water and fire.
Upon the soft breeze, air magick abounds
Embracing the forces within and around.
This magick is worked with harm to none.
So mote it be; there, it is done.

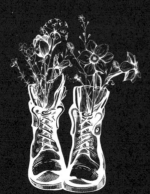

3 Monday

4 Tuesday

5 Wednesday

6 Thursday

Full moon.

7 Friday

Anne Pedersdotter (ca 1530–90), Norwegian witch, burned to death.

8 Saturday

9 Sunday

WITCHERY

Working magickally with the forces of nature involves understanding and reconnecting with elemental magick:

EARTH

logic, goals, common sense, keeping you grounded and stable.

Guardian: gnome.

FIRE

motivating, driving force, strength, courage, passion.

Guardian: salamander.

AIR

aspiration, inspiration, communication, creativity.

Guardian: sylph.

WATER

emotions, intuitive/psychic development, going with the flow.

Guardian: undine.

WITCHY TIP

Bring the beauty and fragrance of flowers into your life by placing them in your home, at work and in your garden and notice how their healing energies, including colour, evoke your senses on every level.

FLOWER FAERY
INCANTATION

I call on the faeries, guardians of flowers
Bestow upon me your magickal powers.
I breathe in the fragrance, filling my heart
Beauty surrounds me, ne'er to depart.
I work with this magick, with harm to none.
To heal and restore me; there, it is done.

10 Monday

11 Tuesday

12 Wednesday

Raven Grimassi (1951–2019), high priest, occultist, wiccan; popularised Stregheria, a religious witchcraft practice.

13 Thursday

Third quarter moon · William Quan Judge (1851–96), occultist and mystic, founder of the Theosophical Society.

14 Friday

15 Saturday

During the Channel Island witch trials from 1550 to 1650 more than 100 people were accused, tortured and executed.

16 Sunday

17   Monday

18   Tuesday

King Olaf Tryggvason of Norway (reigned 995–1000 CE) lured more than 100 pagan magicians into his hall under false pretences and accused them of practising witchcraft. The doors were barred and they were burned; those who escaped were drowned.

19   Wednesday

20   Thursday

New moon.

21   Friday

22   Saturday

23   Sunday

Ursulines de Jésus burned to death in Brazil in 1754 for practising witchcraft.

GLAMOUR MAGICK

It is time to become an enchantress whose abilities to charm, attract and seduce make you a most powerful sorceress and an alluring witch. The femme fatale of witchcraft is manipulating in the extreme, so be sure to cast your illusory spells to ensure an attractive outcome. A deep communion with the fae during this month will draw to you the ability to reflect and magnify all that you wish to attract. Dark beauty secrets, ancient ointments and charms change eye or hair colour and reveal all manner of disguise, as you remember that everything is not what it seems when it comes to the allurement of glamour magick.

GLAMOUR SPELL

Sit in front of a mirror at dusk, and as you brush your hair say:

Alluring spells cast for attraction
Beguiling looks, glamour distraction.
Magick ointment rubbed on eyes
Unveils illusion, reveals all guise.
Peer within, begin to brush
Untangle locks, try not to rush.
Candle to light, gaze into the fire
Image appears, just as you desire.
Outcome revealed through magickal eyes
Witchy reflection of one who is wise.
This magick is now said and done.
So mote it be, with harm to none.

Snuff out the candle and say:

Glamour magick is now cast and done
Perception in place, with harm to none.

24 Monday

25 Tuesday

26 Wednesday

27 Thursday
First quarter moon.

28 Friday

29 Saturday
Titus Livius recorded that in 331 BCE 170 women were executed as witches for causing an epidemic illness in Rome.

30 Sunday

MAY
Hare, milk, bright, willow moon

A celebration of nature in full bloom.

The merry month of May is a celebration of when the energies of nature are at their strongest, for all of life bursts with potent fertility when the goddess is seeded by the god and we witness the conception of new life in full bloom as the start of the summer months to come.

BELTANE: 1 May

GODDESS: Blodeuwedd (Celtic/Welsh), flower face, springtime flowers, new warmth.

MAIDEN: in her fullness, sexuality, sensuality, passion, vitality, consummation.

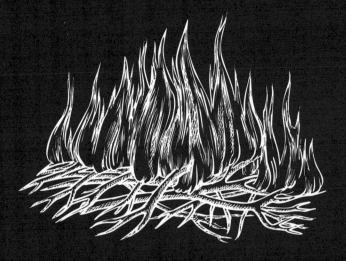

~ BELTANE ~

The maiden has reached her fullness and is the manifestation of growth, sexuality, sensuality, passion, vitality and consummation.

This age-old yearly pagan celebration continues to this day, with villagers gathering to eat together and sip ale as they are treated to traditional Morris dancing and a May queen is chosen. Local children weave ribbons in and out as they dance around a decorated maypole, which represents the traditional rituals that were once held to promote fertility for livestock and people alike.

Traditionally Beltane is a time of the blending of energies of the feminine and masculine, to celebrate the sacredness of sexuality. The goddess takes on the god as her lover in order to give birth to the full bloom of nature during the summer months to come. Beltane marks the return of full life and nature is fully honoured in the fresh bright flowers, grasses and leaves that have started to push through. Think maypoles, a phallic symbol that represents the potency of the god, May queens, flower garlands, handfasting and hawthorn (also known as May trees) and the lords of the Greenwood.

Beltane is celebrated as a fire festival to honour the Celtic sun god Bel. Great fires blazed from the hilltops as a sign of protection and others were lit for couples to leap over hand in hand before running into the woods to consummate their union. It is a time when goals that were set at the beginning of the year come to fruition, when projects take off and relationships bloom. We sow our seeds at Imbolc, and the goddess from her union with her consort gives birth to our goals, dreams and ideas, which spring into reality and continue to grow and blossom.

MAY

1 Monday
Beltane, May Day.

2 Tuesday
Third Witchcraft Act in England in 1604; the instigator was James I.

3 Wednesday

4 Thursday

5 Friday
Full moon.

6 Saturday
Margaret Read burned at the stake in 1590 in King's Lynn, Norfolk.

7 Sunday

BELTANE INCANTATION

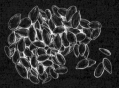

With fires lit across the land
A couple leaps while hand in hand
To mark their union and this rite
For they know tonight's the night!
As they run through darkened wood
And find a grassy glade, they should
Remember well of who's around
For bands of faeries all surround
The couple as they consummate.
The faeries cheer and seal the fate
Of plants and flowers, shrubs and trees
While the god's upon his knees
Impregnating the mother to be
From sowing deep his natural seed.
And so in time the goddess will birth
The magick that's nature on this earth.

WITCH'S WISDOM

It is time to light up your inner world and embrace the power of the flame, for candles highlight the path of the witch to illuminate the way and play a sacred part in Beltane rituals and ceremonies. Witches have a deep affinity with the projective and transformative energy of fire to invoke lust, passion, attraction and love and recognise that flames can be seen across the veil, which is why we light candles for those who have passed over. Lighting candles with the intention of healing, wishes or other purposes enhances your magickal manifestation abilities when it comes to casting spells and bringing about desired results. However, it is vital to remember to keep your thoughts and focus positive when you partake in any wizardry, for that is how true magick is birthed. Never doubt your abilities of focusing, willpower and visualisation, and remember that all is magick and illusion.

WITCHY TIP

The sacred act of candle magick has been with you ever since you blew out your first birthday candle and made a wish. By doing so you worked with the principals of candle wick magick, which makes dreams come true! Scratch your intentions in candle wax with a pin and anoint it with sacred oils for purity of power. Snuff the wick or allow the candle to burn down as you seal the spell. Belief in your tools and yourself when performing any candle magick ritual is vital.

CANDLE INCANTATION

The power of magick comes deep from within
Ignite the flame, let the ritual begin.
Choose colour for purpose, intentions in place
Let light be the focus, desire to embrace.
This magick is worked with harm to none.
So mote it be; there, it is done.

8   Monday

9   Tuesday

Isobel Gowdie, Scottish witch, confessed to practising witchcraft 1662.

10   Wednesday

11   Thursday

12   Friday

Third quarter moon.

13   Saturday

In the first century CE, 80 women were executed for witchcraft in Ashkelon, in Canaan in the Middle East.

14   Sunday

15 Monday

16 Tuesday

17 Wednesday

18 Thursday

Cassandra Latham-Jones was the first person in the United Kingdom to register her work as a witch with the inland revenue, in 1996.

19 Friday

Black moon · A sacred time for harnessing extra power for banishment spells and working with your shadow side.

20 Saturday

21 Sunday

Kitchen witchery

CHILI PEPPER: tap into that untamed, primordial behaviour you have been suppressing. Your savage side screams for you to be raw and unrestrained and to acknowledge your most vehement instincts. Never apologise for being assertive or for striking out to achieve what you want. Instead, the merry month of May requires you to be forceful as you focus on your desires, for the only way to beat the competition and to win right now is to be passionate. As you sprinkle my flakes over dishes I will spice up your life with my intense, powerful pungency. Emotional challenges and ferocious behaviour could leave you red with anger, so feel the intensity of my heat as I spread picante warmth within and feel the burn. You have permission to be fiery, fierce and fabulous!

Witchy recipe

This chili oil is a natural pain reliever, soothes nasal congestion and boosts immunity. Heat 2 tablespoons of your chosen base oil such as olive oil in a pan on medium heat. Add 2 to 3 whole dried red chilies with 2 tablespoons of red chili flakes. Stir the mixture, ensuring the ingredients don't brown. Once sizzling, add a cup of the base oil and continue to heat until the mixture is warmed through, then remove it from the heat. Once cooled, pour the oil into an airtight bottle and store.

Chili pepper: ferocity

String me up, keep me raw
Intense spice could make you sore.
Face the heat, fight fire with fire
Fierce emotions feed desire.
This magick is worked, with harm to none.
So mote it be; there, it is done.

PASSION SPELL

Fire is not to be feared: it's your ticket to full empowerment, fuelling your ability to kindle your true light with full might, vitality and vigour and igniting your magickal power.

Face the direction of south at noon,
light a red candle and say:

Ignite the wick, let the magick begin
Passion fuels the desires within.
Feeling the heat, candles to light
Sacred union, sexual rite.
Allow the fire to ravage through me
To purify, cleanse and set me free.
I am in full power, this I now know
As I become the sacred glow.
Passion and power invoked to reclaim.
Now give thanks and snuff out the flame.

22 Monday

23 Tuesday
Kenneth Grant (1924–2011), ceremonial magician and an advocate of the Thelemic religion.

24 Wednesday

25 Thursday

26 Friday

27 Saturday
First quarter moon.

28 Sunday

JUNE

Moon of horses, hawthorn, strawberry moon

Glorifying the full strength and light of the sun.

June is busting out all over as we celebrate the full bloom of roses, honeysuckle and warmer weather. Named after the Roman goddess Juno, the goddess of marriage, sunny June sees the start of the wedding season, and a June bride is considered to be lucky. June is also the halfway stage of the growing season for farmers, a traditional midpoint between planting and harvesting. The goddess is now the mother, and the sun god is at the height of his virility and life-giving power. Celebrations of fullness, expansiveness and achievements are awash with joy as the light reaches its peak and we enjoy the longest day and shortest night of the wheel of the year.

LITHA: 19-22 June

GODDESS: Áine (Celtic/Irish), faery queen of summer, growth, love, luck and magick.

MOTHER: in her full power and strength.

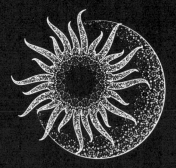

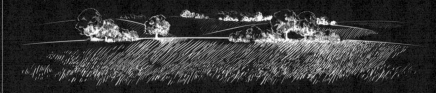

~ LITHA ~

Empowerment, celebration of light and full strength of the sun

This is the month that celebrates the sun festival known as Litha, or the summer solstice, which is when the sun is at its highest point in the sky and is at its strongest. It is a time of intensification, of focus, development and determination as we connect with the sun to become stronger and claim our full self-power in celebration, honour and ritual. Those who are not aware of such connotations still, albeit unwittingly, worship the sun in other ways, partaking in outdoor parties and barbecues and topping up their tans during hot and sunny days.

Celtic tradition, honoured through tales and legends, tells of a great battle that played out at this time of year between the mighty holly king and the majestic oak king. At the summer solstice the holly king won supreme and stood proud through to winter, until at Yule he was cut down in his prime when the oak king won and presided over the coming months until their next battle at Litha.

This is a time of year when you can tap into midsummer magick, for the veil between the worlds is thin. Think a world of Titania, Oberon, faery spells and faery rings of mushrooms, toadstools and flowers in which those with open hearts are invited in to connect with the natural magick of the fae.

29 Monday

30 Tuesday
Joan of Arc, visionary; burned for heresy and witchcraft in 1431.

31 Wednesday

1 Thursday
Fourth Witchcraft Act in England in 1735, instigated by parliament. The act abolished the hunting and execution of witches in the United Kingdom.

2 Friday

3 Saturday

4 Sunday
Full moon.

MIDSUMMER INVOCATION

As I enter within this magical ring
My heart is open and ready to sing
Songs of the wood, words of the fae,
Who guide me in, and show me the way.
I call on the magick of midsummer's eve
Whose mystic and mystery together doth weave.
May power bestow me this very night
As I share my found gifts, for 'tis only right.
With arms outstretched to the magical ones
I give honour and thanks, and so now it's done.

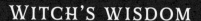

WITCH'S WISDOM

Since the dawn of time witches have observed the summer solstice. It is a time to feel the deep resonance that connects you with this season and to acknowledge a heightened sense of awareness for the rhythms and rituals that take place at this intense time. Be still to embrace each moment as you notice the change in all of nature: look to the trees, embrace the landscape and observe the sun in its momentum of strength. The same is true for you when you stand in a sacred circle or at a sacred site to mark Litha: you are one with the ancient ancestors, the spirits of the land, and the power of the place on which you stand.

Sabbats provide natural pauses in the wheel of the year, a time to breathe and reflect in deep gratitude and celebration. Witches harness the elemental forces of nature and work with them in honour of the mother aspects of the triple goddess in relation to this season and a celebration of the sun. It's time to take a deep breath and immerse yourself in the physical and spiritual effects this time of year offers, to become one with the cycles of nature in balance and harmony. Celebration time is upon you now as you count your blessings, honour all you have sown and give thanks to the faeries and nature spirits, and emerge through dance and song or whatever fuels your strength, passion and love of nature.

✶ INCANTATION

A celebration of goddess, from maiden to mother
Farewell spring months, summer offers another.
The sun in ascent fuels passion and strength
Standing stones honour all rituals at length.
This magick is worked with harm to none.
So mote it be; there, it is done.

5 Monday

6 Tuesday

Alex Sanders (1926–88), occulist and high priest, founder of Alexandrian wicca.

7 Wednesday

Swein Macdonald (1931–2003), highland seer, mystic and occultist.

8 Thursday

9 Friday

10 Saturday

Third quarter moon · First hangings of witches at Gallows Hill, Salem, Massachusetts. Bridget Bishop was the first witch to hang, in 1692.

11 Sunday

12 Monday

13 Tuesday
Gerald Gardner (1884–1964), high priest, founder of Gardnerian wicca.

14 Wednesday

15 Thursday
Muree bin Ali bin Issa al-Asiri, beheaded for witchcraft in Saudi Arabia in 2012.

16 Friday

17 Saturday

18 Sunday
New moon.

Kitchen Witchery

GINGER: if you've found that your magickal abilities have waned lately or wish to add more piquancy to your spell work then allow me to assist. My forceful and fiery influence will help to accelerate the results you desire, for the power of my root has been revered since ancient times. When someone tries to overshadow you and you are down or bullied your personal power fades. Add some ginger magick into your world and turn up the heat! I will bring you confidence so you can live up to your full potential. As your power increases, together we shall combat nightmares, incite passion and heal physical ailments such as stomach and digestive problems. My medicinal properties offer anti-inflammatory and antioxidant effects and spice up your culinary delights in the kitchen, intensifying your inner strength and fuelling your power.

Ginger: power

My knobbly root turns up the heat
Add to dishes, a spicy treat.
Lack of zeal has left you sour
Now stand strong, be in your power.
This magick is worked, with harm to none.
So mote it be; there, it is done.

Witchy recipe

This ginger tonic will relieve heartburn, motion sickness and colds and flu. Add 1 cup of minced ginger root to ¾ cup of filtered/spring water, bring to the boil and simmer for two hours. Let the tonic cool then add the juice of 3 lemons, a pinch of sea salt and your favourite spices. Strain into a jar and refrigerate. This is a concentrate, so dilute it to taste and add a slice of lemon.

EMPOWERMENT SPELL

Write one word each on separate pieces of paper that represents self-empowerment so you can draw it to yourself under the solstice sun, such as strength, vigour, might, potential, power and so on.

Light a gold candle and safely burn each piece of paper in the flame in turn, then say:

*To empower my life bring me the same
As I set you alight in this solar bright flame.*

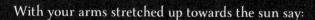

With your arms stretched up towards the sun say:

*A path that glitters is revealed
Follow, for my fate is sealed.
Seek, unlock the truth this noon
Inner strength intensified soon.
Gratefully I accept the magick of sun
Of strength to assist in all said and done.
Shine through me brightly, build power in me
Assist my transcendence. So mote it be.*

19 Monday

20 Tuesday

21 Wednesday
Litha, summer solstice, midsummer.

22 Thursday

23 Friday

24 Saturday

25 Sunday

26 Monday
First quarter moon.

27 Tuesday
Scott Cunningham (1956–93), wrote about wicca and herbalism.

28 Wednesday

29 Thursday
Today in India women are still labelled as witches in order to take their lands, settle scores or punish them for not accepting sexual advances. It is estimated that between 50 and 100 women are killed as witches each year.

30 Friday

1 Saturday
Witchcraft Act in England repealed in 1951 and replaced with the Fraudulent Mediums Act.

2 Sunday

JULY

Hay, thunder, mead, oak moon

The power of summer burns brightly, intensifying passion and destiny.

The month of July signifies the height of summer in all its glorious radiance, as the sun beats down upon the optimum abundance of nature's full bloom. Now is the time to enjoy the gifts of the mother goddess, for your work is done.

The magick of summer invites intense energies of lust, passion, attraction, illumination, love, sex, sun and heat. Put down your tools, have fun and enjoy the carefree days of summer, as taking a well-deserved break to rejuvenate is essential for your well-being on all levels. Be careful not to get burned while you enjoy outdoor parties, barbecues and sunbathing during this hot, passionate month as you worship the sun and harness the power of the element of fire. In magickal terms the intensity of high noon is a perfect time to cast spells while facing the direction of south. As the heat of the sun breathes renewed passion into your workings and relationships you attract the energy of abundance, awakening your spiritual kundalini energy through lust, attraction and desire as you draw down the sun.

As the sun greets you it highlights the path you are to take towards your destiny, in order for you to complete your life's mission.

GODDESS: **Étaín (Celtic/Irish),** the shining one, sun and moon goddess, lights the way on the path of transformation towards balance, wholeness and rebirth.

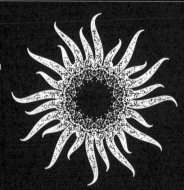

MOTHER: uncovering the light and strength within, beauty, sun, love, vitality of life.

SUMMER INCANTATION

Ignite the passion of summer and know
You are the power, the sacred glow.
Love and passion stirred and invoked
Abundance is yours now the fire is stoked.
Lounging, bronzing in the sun
Sea salt air and having fun.
Food delights, cocktails too
Take this well-earned break, for you
To be restored, take the charge.
Enjoy the rest now. Bon voyage!

MOON MAGICK

Flowers are in full bloom and honey is fermenting, and it is a busy bee who pollinates their ideas and dreams. There are no limits when it comes to sweet success; devotion to the bigger picture serves your projects well, and you'll soon be enjoying the fruits of your hard labour. As the mead moon shines its honeyed beam upon these warm nights, draw from its powers of prosperity. As you take a sip from the amber nectar of the gods make plans to gather together the ingredients you need to move forward, for everything you require is ripe for the picking. A community built on firm foundations is key when it comes to sharing with others, so instead of flitting in between projects allow the intoxicating and heady energy of the mead moon to support and ground you even if others are trying to clip your wings.

3 Monday
Full moon.

4 Tuesday

5 Wednesday
Lucy Cavendish (1961–), bestselling author, witch and druid.

6 Thursday

7 Friday

8 Saturday

9 Sunday

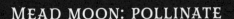

MEAD MOON: POLLINATE

Drink of the moon on this warm night
Pollinate with goals in sight.
Oh, mead of honey, golden hue
Your sweet success I shall pursue,
This magick is worked with harm to none.
So mote it be; there, it is done.

WITCHY TIPS

Make honey cakes and drink mead in honour of the mother goddess, place a chalice of mead on your altar and wear bee jewellery or amulets to attract prosperity. A bee brings prosperity when it enters your home. The goddess Brigid's familiar was a bee, and they are held sacred for their magickal nectar.

KITCHEN WITCHERY

HONEY: allow me to help you out of the sticky situation you've fallen into as I add a little sweetness into your life. I am food for the gods, the celestial nectar, and I have been worshipped for thousands of years by almost every culture for my amber-hued delights. Drizzle me over baked goods or stir me into a hot drink to eliminate the bitter taste in the mouth you've experienced lately. Keep going, as your hard work will pay off just as it does for the honeybees, who work tirelessly. My golden liquid has graced royal tables from breakfast to dinner in the forms of honey and mead. It is time for a little honey magick, so add me as a magickal ingredient to spells for my potency magnifies results. My cleansing, healing and antiseptic powers depict immortality, and I guarantee the longevity of success for you as you take a taste of ambrosia.

HONEY: AMBROSIA

Food for the gods, liquid delight
Spread me at breakfast, drink me at night.
Taste of ambrosia, sugary sweet
Honey bee nectar, magickal treat.
This magick is worked, with harm to none.
So mote it be; there, it is done.

WITCHY RECIPE

This honey salve is great for wounds and infection; it uses equal parts of olive oil, raw natural honey and beeswax.
Melt beeswax in a double boiler then stir in honey and olive oil. Add a few pinches of turmeric or a spice of your choice. Cool to room temperature, adding in extra beeswax or oil until the desired texture has been reached.

10 Monday

Third quarter moon.

11 Tuesday

12 Wednesday

13 Thursday

Margaret Murray (1863–1963), Egyptologist, archaeologist, occultist and folklorist; the first woman to be appointed as a lecturer in a university, in 1898 · John Dee (1527–1608), court astronomer to Elizabeth I of England, occultist, alchemist and mystic.

14 Friday

15 Saturday

16 Sunday

17 Monday

New moon · Chelmsford Assizes, a periodic court for serious crime and witch trials in Essex, England · Elizabeth Francis (1529-79) convicted three times for betwitchment and witchcraft; she was executed after the third trial.

18 Tuesday

19 Wednesday

Second hangings of the Salem witches in the United States; five women were executed in 1692.

20 Thursday

21 Friday

22 Saturday

Mother Agnes Waterhouse (1503-66), the first woman to be executed in England for witchcraft.

23 Sunday

HOLIDAY SPELL

Hold a small bag and imagine packing it with all you require for a trip. Face the direction of south at noon and say:

I leave behind my comfort zone
Security and all I own.
No time to waste sitting inside
Time to venture far and wide.
Decision made to go seek fun
To bathe, explore, enjoy the sun.
Where to travel? Contemplation
Surprises point to destination.

Wrap a cord thrice around your bag and say:

Gratefully I accept your magick today
Of protection to assist me on my way.

JULY

24 Monday

25 Tuesday
First quarter moon.

26 Wednesday

27 Thursday
Pendle witch trials started in 1612 in the York Assizes, a periodic court for serious crime and witch trials.

28 Friday
Huntingdon Assizes, a periodic court for serious crime and witch trials; Mary Hicks, a witch of Huntingdon, and her nine-year-old daughter were both hanged for witchcraft in 1716.

29 Saturday
Jennet Preston hanged in 1612 at York Racecourse · Sarah Good hanged with four other woman from the Salem witch trials in 1692.

30 Sunday

AUGUST

Corn, holly, grain moon

Celebration and gratitude of the grain harvest.

This heady month of sun and fun is greeted as a time of opportunity and good fortune, for these are the carefree days of summer when the dreams that were seeded at Imbolc come fully into fruition and are now ripe for the picking. We witness the first hint of autumn as the hottest part of summer makes its promise to wane, through its shortened days and the first grains ready to be harvested. It's time to reap the harvest of rewards and appreciate and bless everything that comes our way, as we make the most of the remaining light and warm weather before autumn and give thanks for the abundance of the growth of the passing season.

LUGHNASADH: 1 August

GODDESS: **Tailtiu (Celtic/Irish)**, goddess of August and of the earth, the harvest and first grains; she is the foster mother of the sun god Lugh.

MOTHER: matures, gratitude for earthly, physical sustenance.

~ Lughnasadh ~

Gratitude for the gifts of the earth

Lughnasadh marks the very first harvest of the year and the gathering in of the grains. It is when the sun god Lugh – who is also known as John Barleycorn, Jack in the Green and Robin Hood – is celebrated as he is cut down in his prime, only to rise up again the following year. This is an important and busy time of year that our ancestors looked forward to, a time of plenty when there was feasting in celebration of the first harvest and to honour the natural cycle of life, death and rebirth, represented as the spirit of John Barleycorn. His time will come again, but for now the seeds planted earlier in the year have grown into an abundant crop and are ready to be harvested and stored in the grain barns to see out the cold and barren months to come.

LUGHNASADH INVOCATION

Today the wheel of the year doth stop
At Lughnasadh, time to reap the crops
That were sown earlier this year.
Celebrate the harvest cheer
Of wheat, of cereal, of the grain
Store it safely, before the wane.
John Barleycorn is now cut down,
From his prime, but look around
For Lugh the sun god shines from high,
Over the fields from the sky.
From Mother Earth we are blessed,
Toil now over, soon can rest.
But from the sow, what did you reap?
Is it good, or do you weep?
From hard work what have you earned?
Of the lesson, what is learned?
May the magick of this day
Bless you now in every way.

31 Monday

1 Tuesday
Full moon · Lughnasadh/Lammas.

2 Wednesday

3 Thursday

4 Friday

5 Saturday
Malin Matsdotter (1613–76), originally from Sweden and of Finnish descent, was burned as a witch.

6 Sunday

WITCH'S WISDOM

Fire-loving witches enjoy bronzing under the sun as they worship its strength in the form of sunbathing, for they know how vital exposure to sunlight is for boosting mood, sleep and bones.

However, those whose witchy hearts feel the allure of moon magick prefer to bathe under its soft, feminine glow, for the moon is the keeper of magick, of mystery, of beauty and divine feminine energies and invites you to benefit from its silver stream of magickal offerings this month. As you call down the moon she embraces you in her soft, luminous glow. Bathe in the pure feminine and restorative energy she immerses you with and go sky clad in honour of the triple goddess. As you open up to your receptive feminine side and honour the mother goddess for her gifts at this time of year, abundance will seek you out.

GRAIN MOON: HARVESTING

The harvest's in, moon of grain
Mother Earth provides again.
Rewards to reap, goals to complete
Gratitude for corn and wheat.
This magick is now said and done.
So mote it be, with harm to none.

KITCHEN WITCHERY

PATCHOULI: don't give up even if you feel your life has no meaning or direction, for I am here to change your outlook and remind you that having a purpose enables you to live life to the fullest. Seize the day and embrace your ideas to achieve your goals and reignite your passion, and I shall give you good reasons to get up in the mornings. Use me in meditation as I transport your mind to far-off magical places with just one sniff of my musky and exotic scent. My potency will evoke nostalgic memories for your soul to awaken and remind you why you are here on this beautiful planet at this time. Anoint your doors and windows with oil as a magical defence or to repel negative influences, and use me in spells and rituals to attain the spiritual growth you've been seeking as well as mastery of the self.

WITCHY RECIPE

This foot cream is great for athlete's foot, eczema and dermatitis.
Put 50 millilitres each of fractionated coconut oil, almond oil and melted shea butter in a double boiler and gently heat. Add 25 to 30 drops of patchouli oil and then cool in the fridge. When the mixture has set, whisk it up with a hand blender. Stir in a handful of chopped patchouli flowers, put it into jars and store in the fridge.

PATCHOULI: PURPOSE

This sacred path is yours to own
Set personal goals for you alone.
My potent oil will help achieve
Direction, purpose. Now believe.
This magick is worked, with harm to none.
So mote it be; there, it is done.

AUGUST

7   Monday

8   Tuesday
Third quarter moon.

9   Wednesday
Akua Denteh was beaten to death for practising witchcraft in Ghana on 9 August 2020.

10 Thursday
World Day against Witch Hunts created after Akua Denteh was killed
in Ghana.

11 Friday

12 Saturday
Madame Helena Blavatsky (1831-91), Russian occultist, philosopher and co-founder of the
Theosophical Society.

13 Sunday

14 Monday

15 Tuesday

16 Wednesday
New moon.

17 Thursday

18 Friday
Pendle and Samlesbury witch trials held in 1612 at the Lancaster Assizes; nine women and one man found guilty of witchcraft.

19 Saturday
Salem witch trials held in the United States in 1692: one woman and five men hung for witchcraft.

20 Sunday
Pendle witches hanged in 1612 at Gallows Hill in Lancaster, United Kingdom.

PROSPERITY SPELL

Take a small pin, anoint patchouli oil onto a green candle,
hold a coin in your left hand and say:

Coin of abundance I ask for new peace
From poverty, debt, I wish for release.
Carve owed amount on candle green
Anoint with oil to pay bills foreseen.
Debt's now reduced as candle burns
Flame to determine what one earns.
Watch arrears now melt away
Welcoming in a new fat pay day.
Prosperity's mine and the chance to succeed
Adorned now with riches, I have more than I need.

Watch the entire candle burn down to banish debt completely
and then bury the coin in the earth so that prosperity and
abundance can grow in your life.

21   Monday

22   Tuesday

23   Wednesday

24   Thursday
First quarter moon.

25   Friday

26   Saturday

27   Sunday

28 Monday

29 Tuesday

30 Wednesday

31 Thursday

Blue moon: an auspicious day to cast spells and magickal rituals for knowledge and wisdom ·
Raymond Buckland (1934-2017), high priest and occultist.

1 Friday

First laws on spells and witchcraft passed in the Code of Hammurabi from 1754 BCE in
ancient Mesopotamia.

2 Saturday

3 Sunday

SEPTEMBER

Harvest, hazel, fruit, barley moon

A time for gathering, resting, reflecting and celebration.

As the cycle of the natural world moves further towards completion in the wheel of the year, we find ourselves on the cusp of transition just before the year begins to wane into darkness. Following the celebration of the grain harvest at Lughnasadh, which is now fully in and stored, we acknowledge the abundance and ripeness of the fruits of the earth the harvest queen bestows upon us at this time of year. The goddess is found in her mother aspect in the fading summer twilight or in the harvest moon.

As the full life of summer comes to an end we become witness to ripe fruits, nuts, squashes and the flaming autumn colours of red, orange and gold as nature turns in on herself with the promise of the darker barren months of winter to come. This was a time of preparation, gathering and storing for our ancestors, as the final harvest of fruits and vegetables was brought in to last through the winter months. Traditionally workers were paid for the upcoming year, annual dues were collected and accounts were balanced. As autumnal mists descend, soft ripe fruit falls gently from the heavily laden trees that fill the glade. Nature's gifts are in abundance as the soft autumnal sun declines and autumnal mists descend. It is time to celebrate and draw from the earth's bounty.

MABON: 21 September

GODDESS: Banbha (Celtic/Irish), earth mother, protection, fruitfulness, keeper of mystery.

MOTHER: contemplation, self-sufficiency and balance.

~ MABON ~

When day and night is in balance and the fruit harvest is celebrated.

Mabon is a recent name that has been adopted by witches and pagans alike to celebrate the autumn equinox, when daylight and darkness are in balance with each other and night and day are of equal length and in perfect equilibrium; there is dark and light, masculine and feminine, inner and outer. The name 'Mabon' is associated with the Welsh god of mythology, Mabon, and also with the faery queen Mab, who rules over the Unseelie Court of autumn and winter.

At this time of balance and celebration we are reminded that we too are a part of nature. This is a time of going deep within, of resting after the labour of harvest, and a time for reflection and to count our blessings for the abundance that has been bestowed upon us throughout the year thus far. We must look at where we have been and what has been done during the preceding months and give thanks, which in turn will truly fill both our inner and outer gifts. This is when you reap what you had sown earlier in the year and harvest all that's now been made manifest from your earlier dreams and aspirations. It's a good time to let go of all that is no longer necessary and watch it fall away, just as the leaves do at this time of year. As you acknowledge and embrace your shadow side, bring it into balance with the light that you already exude. Draw from the power of the cornucopia of abundance, a symbol for the wealth of harvest at Mabon, and balance your masculine and feminine energies so that you can be both giving and receptive at this time of year.

4   Monday

5   Tuesday

6   Wednesday
Third quarter moon.

7   Thursday
Margaret Ine Quaine and John Cubbon executed in Castletown, Isle of Man in 1617. There is a memory plaque on Smelt Monument.

8   Friday

9   Saturday

10   Sunday
Tiberius Claudius, emperor from 41 to 54 CE, executed 45 men and 85 women for witchcraft.

MABON INCANTATION

Autumn's upon us, here at last.
A time to reflect upon the past
Of the year that seems to have flown.
Dreams were planted now have grown.
Mabon gifts us dark and light
Of perfect balance both day and night.
And so we look deep down within
To check our equilibrium.
Look back on past hurts, lessons learned.
And use them so you won't get burned.
Important to shine out far and wide
And to honour shadow side
For both together makes you whole
The two as one completes your soul.
Light two candles, one black, one white
Representing your joy and plight.
Eliminate all you do not need
But keep what you have to succeed.
The harvest's in, we give great cheer
And thanks for an abundant year.

MOON MAGICK

The juicy full September moon bestows upon you a bountiful harvest, when nature's fruit bowl is at its ripest. It is time to bathe in the hue of colours, of the red and orange that decorate the autumnal sky at sunset. As the luscious fruit falls from the trees you'll find some will be left to rot and decay, such is the process of death. Fill up your inner fruit bowl, for an inexhaustible supply of what you require is yours as you take up witchy arms in ritual and thanksgiving. The fruit harvest is in, and it's time to reap the bumper crop you've been focusing on. Times are sweet when the fruit moon appears on the horizon, so take a deep breath and immerse yourself in the magickal effects that this time of year offers. Celebration is upon you as a bountiful supply of abundance is all yours for the taking, in balance and gratitude.

FRUIT MOON: BOUNTIFUL

Ripe for the picking, fruits to yield
Bumper crop, abundance sealed.
Celebrate the harvest, vast
Fruitful batch now reaped to last.
This magick is now said and done.
So mote it be, with harm to none.

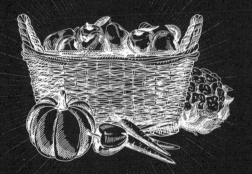

SEPTEMBER

11 Monday

Silver RavenWolf (1956–), author of many books on witchcraft and wicca.

12 Tuesday

13 Wednesday

14 Thursday

15 Friday

New moon.

16 Saturday

17 Sunday

18   Monday

19   Tuesday

Fulda witch trials in Germany between 1603 and 1606. Merga Bien (1560-1603) burned alive.

20   Wednesday

21   Thursday

Mabon, the autumn equinox.

22   Friday

First quarter moon · Salem witch trials in the United States between 1692 and 1693; eight people hanged for witchcraft.

23   Saturday

24   Sunday

North Berwick witch trials in the United Kingdom between 1590 and 1592; more than 70 people were implicated.

WITCH'S WISDOM

You are called to become more self-reliant and self-supporting, for it is key to your survival, just as the witches of old had to plan their survival by storing grain for the winter months: it was a matter of life or death. However, forget supermarket stockpiling and instead try the hedgerow aisles, where all good food grows for free. Grab a bag, don thick gloves and take your pick from nourishing nettles to sweet chestnuts, red rosehips and sumptuous blackberries. For many witches, foraging compels a greater awareness of their surroundings as they seek natural ingredients for ingestion and medicinal purposes, so seek out wild edibles and pick sumptuous berries in balance and gratitude. Foraging will deepen your connection with the natural world and will keep you in tune with the seasons. Go into nature and allow the fruits of the earth to restore you as you feast from nature's table.

INCANTATION

Sloes for gin or wicked jelly
Crab apples, nuts, to fill your belly.
Tasty treats both wild and free
Be self-reliant; 'tis the key.
This magick is worked with harm to none.
So mote it be; there, it is done.

WITCHY TIP

DANDELION: eat raw or cooked leaves and the root or make tea with the dried leaves. Dandelion is packed with vitamins A, K, C and E, calcium, iron and manganese.

WILD GARLIC: both the flowers and bulb are edible. Use wild garlic in soups and salads and for sauces.

ELDERFLOWER: packed with vitamin C, use elderflower to make a healing herbal tea or delicious elderflower cordial. It is a good remedy for hay fever and coughs.

BLACKBERRY: high in vitamins C and K and manganese and delicious in crumbles and pies.

NETTLE: enriched with calcium, manganese, magnesium and iron. Always soak the leaves first to denature the sting, then eat young leaves raw or cooked for soup to detox the blood and clear uric acid.

25 Monday

26 Tuesday
Witch-hunts are still being inflicted upon innocent women and men today, from Sub-Saharan Africa, India, the Middle East, the Amazon and Papua New Guinea.

27 Wednesday

28 Thursday

29 Friday
Full moon.

30 Saturday

1 Sunday
It is estimated that over 200,000 witches were burned or hanged in Western Europe.

WITCHY RECIPE

The mid-autumn festival or at the time of a full moon is when mooncakes are traditionally baked and eaten, for lunar appreciation and moon gazing. Combine 2 tablespoons of butter with 3 tablespoons of sugar, 3 tablespoons of plain flour, 3 tablespoons of rolled oats, ½ teaspoon of vanilla essence and 1 tablespoon of cream. Bake at 190°C for 20 minutes in honour of the moon and in gratitude. Leave on your altar or enjoy the mooncakes in ritual. Gratitude is a guaranteed recipe for success!

GRATITUDE BALANCE SPELL

Light an orange candle, face west and say:

Complain and moan, no gratitude
Won't serve me well, 'tis plainly rude.
Release all judgement, keep heart light
Scales of Mabon weigh all blight.
So I'll give thanks for each great gift
Balance gained, as shadows shift.
Equilibrium, light and dark
Fairness chosen to embark.
Kitchen witch, it's time to bake
Moon rites honour, eat some cake!

Write down all that you are grateful for.
Place the list under a lit candle and let the candle safely burn down to receive manifest goodness in your life.

October

Blood, vine, hunter's moon

Season of witches, the olde Celtic year dies.

October is the month when we witness the death of nature. As leaves continue to fall we enjoy the vibrant colours of the season, an abundance of squashes and darker nights. Now that the harvest is in and was celebrated at Mabon it's a time to prepare fruit jam preserves and tinctures for colds and flu, using ingredients collected from the earth, trees and hedgerows such as rose hips, apples and berries. The crone, who reigns over the harsher months, is cold and callous and now beckons you with a bony finger to witness the death of nature and all that will assist you in moving forward.

SAMHAIN: 31 October

GODDESS: Cerridwen (Celtic/Welsh), keeper of the gates between the worlds, grail goddess.

CRONE: bringer of darkness and death, of blood and bone and the underworld.

~ SAMHAIN ~

An honouring of the souls of the dead,
when the veil between the worlds is thinnest.

Hallowe'en conjures up ghosts, pumpkin lanterns and children shouting 'Trick or treat!' as they hungrily hold out bags for candy. It is celebrated at the end of October. Traditionally called Samhain, this is an old Celtic celebration of summer's end. Fires were lit on the night of 31 October and villagers would burn crops and animals to their gods and goddesses to share with them and to give thanks for the bounty of the harvest. The Celts believed that the souls of the dead in the underworld were set free for that night, some of whom were welcomed and others feared. Costumes and masks were worn for protection from these spirits. The veil between the worlds at this time is at its thinnest, so we are more able to see and connect with the world of faery and spirit.

Samhain is still considered to be a time of connection and reflection on those who have left this world for the other, and to look at where we have journeyed from and to during the wheel of the year. The goddess in her triple form has become the crone, and we are invited to draw on her wisdom from deep within as she cradles us during the dark months to come, enabling us to release all that no longer serves us.

2 Monday

Arthur Edward Waite (1857–1942), occultist, magician, alchemist and co-creator of the Rider-Waite tarot.

3 Tuesday

4 Wednesday

5 Thursday

6 Friday

Third quarter moon.

7 Saturday

8 Sunday

SAMHAIN INCANTATION

Cauldrons are boiling, lanterns are shining
Ghouls and ghosts, groans and whining.
Parties sweep across the land
Children, adults, hand in hand.
Time of fun but must remember
As fires burn bright and glow with embers
Our ancestors who walked before.
We honour thee and ask for more
Wisdom, tools, to help us be.
The wise among us, let us see,
Through veil, while thin, this very night
Protection in place, no need for fright.
We welcome you and all you bring.
Go deep inside and look within
To shed the old, a shamanic death
Embraced and warmed within the earth.
Inviting in life anew
The goddess calls for it to be you.
Through the year from maiden to mother
The end is now, to feel the other.
In her glory stands the crone
Don't be afraid to stand alone.
This sacred path leads you to be free
Go forth in strength. So mote it be.

WITCH'S WISDOM

When the crone is exposed you should be careful not to be drawn into the shadows, for this is where the darkness seems most inviting. The crone is the mistress of magick, the all-powerful sorceress who summons up the power from all that she is. All things in nature have a darker side, which is essential when it comes to transformation and should not be avoided for light can only be seen through the darkness. Both have a necessary purpose and cannot exist without the other. Allow the crone to envelop her dark cloak around you, for it is the only way for you to truly see. She will teach you how to draw strength from the dark mystery and claim the force and power that reside in the shadows of death and endings. There is no turning back when the crone walks with you. However, do not fear; instead, be ready to emerge, to be transformed and hold the energy of both dark and light in balance, knowing and wisdom.

INCANTATION

In her glory stands the crone
Be not afraid to stand alone.
New life poised upon my breath
As transformation invites in death.
This magick is worked with harm to none.
So mote it be; there, it is done.

OCTOBER

9 Monday
Flavia Kate Peters (1968–), high priestess, faery seer, occultist, United Kingdom.

10 Tuesday

11 Wednesday

12 Thursday
Aleister Crowley (1875–1947), English occultist, high priest, ceremonial magician.

13 Friday
All Templars living in France in 1307 were arrested and condemned for witchcraft and heresy. This is often inaccurately cited as the origin of Friday the 13th being unlucky.

14 Saturday
New moon · Patricia Crowther (1927–), early mother of modern wicca, high priestess, United Kingdom.

15 Sunday

16 Monday

17 Tuesday

18 Wednesday

19 Thursday

20 Friday

Selena Fox (1949-), wiccan priestess and pagan elder.

21 Saturday

22 Sunday

First quarter moon · Witch trials were held in Torsåker, Sweden in 1674 and 1675; 71 people were beheaded and burned as witches.

PROTECTION

When darker, malevolent forces gather and things go awry a witch is in vital need of magickal protection. Over the centuries witches have been subjected to hostility, vindictiveness and good old-fashioned jealousy when it comes to harnessing magickal power and casting spells.

Whenever you cast spells or work a little witchery it is vitally important that you protect yourself. In fact, it is good practice to call in protection every day whether you are consciously working magickally or not. The responsibility is yours to place much needed protection around yourself, as without it you are wide open to psychic attack and have nothing in place to defend your energy field. Wearing a hag stone as a pendant around your neck as an amulet of protection is recommended, as it will connect you with all the endurance qualities you need to face down and banish darker days.

HAG STONE: PROTECTION

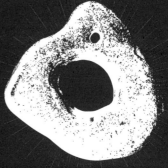

Protective power from witching stone
Defending my path, as I stand alone.
Now out of danger, protection in place
Magical work is safe to embrace.
This magick is worked with harm to none.
So mote it be; there, it is done.

ANCESTORS

The ancestors should be honoured at this time, as understanding the ways of those who've walked before you will help you to release any hurts and pains. Healing ancestral lines enables you to break free of the past. Remember who you are and where you have come from. Your blood ancestors pass on great teachings as well as love, nurture and support, so call out their names in ritual to heal past hurts. Forgiveness is key for moving forward, so all ancestral lines can be cleared. Light candles for those who have gone before you in honour and gratitude.

'We are the bones of your bones, the blood flowing through your veins pulsing with the rhythmic beat of ancient wisdom. You are never alone, for we watch over you and protect you always.'

INCANTATION

Ancestors of blood and bone
Of those remembered and unknown.
Ancient past found in reflection
Honouring a deep connection.
This magick is worked with harm to none
So mote it be; there, it is done.

23 Monday

24 Tuesday

Over 2,000 magickal books were burned by the Emperor Augustus of Rome in 31 BCE.

25 Wednesday

26 Thursday

27 Friday

28 Saturday

Full moon.

29 Sunday

KITCHEN WITCHERY

YARROW: put your boundaries in place and expel anything that is preventing you from being your magical best. Richly endowed with spiritual properties, I've been preserved in temples and treated with reverence for my ability to influence life blood and people's essence, which is carried through the blood itself. As an amulet I will protect against evil, for my power is capable of overcoming the forces of darkness. I will safeguard you from the toxic behaviour of others. Keep in mind that I intensify the work of other herbs and increase their essential oil content. Do not be fooled by my pretty lace features, for I'll make you sweat to break a fever and have the power to ostracise congestion, bruises, arthritis and measles. Plant me next to your threshold so I can deport fearsome spirits, eject any poisonous plants that infect your herb garden and banish any other toxins that creep into your life.

WITCHY RECIPE

This powder is great for nose bleeds and wounds. Harvest yarrow leaves only, not the flowers. If you hang them up to dry, use the long leaves at the bottom of the plant, and if you are using a dehydrator use the base leaves or the leaves of the stem. Once the herbs are dried place the leaves in a coffee or herb grinder and grind to a fine powder. Keep the powder in a dry place in an airtight container.

YARROW: EXPULSION

Fever's high, I'll sweat it out
Toxins exiled, there's no doubt.
Expulsion is my forceful charm
As I dismiss and expel harm.
This magick is worked, with harm to none.
So mote it be; there, it is done.

PROTECTION SPELL

Sprinkle a circle of salt around you, light a black candle and face a dark moon. Raise your arms to the crone and say out loud:

All hail dark moon this very night
Protection placed, no need for fright.
In her glory stands the crone
I'm not afraid to stand alone.
I welcome you and all you bring
Fears to face, journey within.
My ancestors, who walked before
I honour thee, now I am sure.
This sacred path will set me free.
With harm to none; so mote it be.

Deeply breathe in the dark moon as you hold the black candle. Allow a recalibration as you become attuned to the energy of the crone goddess, enabling you to connect with the transformation she offers at Samhain.

NOVEMBER

Snow, ivy, dark moon

Reassessment, embracing loss and acceptance.

Happy New Year! After the death of the year that we witnessed at Samhain, 1 November is celebrated by witches as All Hallows' Day, the start of the Celtic new year and the beginning of winter. However, November is regarded as being an autumnal month that offers a mix of cold and bright, as burned orange leaves continue to fall in the now rather chilly northern hemisphere. The weather can be confusing with its bright sunshine accompanying much colder days, which bring with them the promise of hard frost and sometimes snow. These harsh, biting days are a good time to defend yourself and define your boundaries with others and for using darker magick to ward off harm.

However, as we prepare to face the harshness of winter yet to come we can rejoice in a month of festivities, of thanksgiving, fireworks and remembrance. It is a time of rain and great storms and thus a good time for weather witching!

GODDESS: **the Morrighan (Celtic/Irish)**, battle goddess of death and war, bane magick and darker arts.

CRONE: death and rebirth, sovereignty, inner strength.

WEATHER MAGICK

Raising gusts of wind, summoning lightning and driving in torrential rain will blow all those who vex you off course, for the signs that you've weathered many storms are clear and you are urged to take charge of a tempestuous situation that's been brewing of late. Instead of being influenced by the chaotic, unpredictable forces of nature and caught up in the drama of life's challenges, it's time to be centred and still in the eye of the storm.

Weather witches naturally understand that with a little manipulation a desired result can always be magickally attained. From divination and providing fair winds at sea to raising or preventing treacherous storms, weather witches have the invaluable skill of being able to control and manipulate the weather as well as predict it. If you've ever tried to whistle up a wind or blow up a storm with purposeful breath, then the turbulent influence of another may easily be controlled too as you reclaim your natural power as a weather witch.

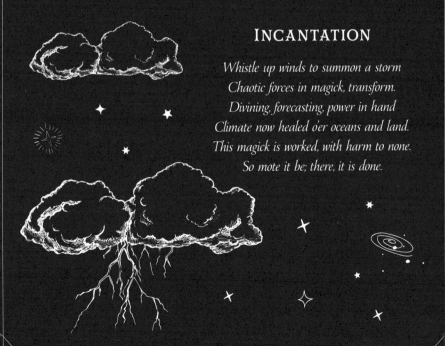

INCANTATION

Whistle up winds to summon a storm
Chaotic forces in magick, transform.
Divining, forecasting, power in hand
Climate now healed o'er oceans and land.
This magick is worked, with harm to none.
So mote it be; there, it is done.

30 Monday

31 Tuesday

Samhain, Hallowe'en · A time to honour the ancestors who have gone before us in the name of witchcraft who have been persecuted, burned, drowned, hanged and stoned.

1 Wednesday

In 331 BCE over 170 women were executed in Rome for witchcraft.

2 Thursday

3 Friday

Petronilla de Meath (1300-24) was burned at the stake in Kilkenny, Ireland. This was the first known case in Ireland and the United Kingdom of death by fire for heresy.

4 Saturday

5 Sunday

Third quarter moon.

MOON MAGICK

Dabbling in destructive workings in all aspects of sorcery, theatrical ceremony and ritual magick for harmful purposes is certain to come back on you. Hexing, banishing and binding are, of course, uncanny gifts of a witch but they should be used wisely. As turbulent, unsettling times reach a climax, chaos heralds the gift of deliverance in many forms as you recover from or face destruction and despair. The blackness of the dark moon reveals shadows, but instead of cloaking your supernatural senses ask the crone to protect you through these darkened months, for she is the mistress of magick who rules the dark moon. It is she who holds the keys to the great mystery of life, death and rebirth and the transformation she offers you now as you surrender to the darkness.

INCANTATION

Hubble, bubble, cast out trouble
Hex and vex all, on the double.
Destruction, death of all you've known
'Tis the dark gift of the crone.
This moon magick is said and done.
So mote it be, with harm to none.

KITCHEN WITCHERY

GARLIC: when you're feeling vexed by unwanted and all-consuming energies it's time to invite some raw garlic into your kitchen. Sprinkle me in dishes and place me above your door, in poppets or around your neck and I will rid you of malevolent spirits, demonic possession and anyone who is draining your very life force. My history is steeped in Eastern European folklore although I go back much further than that, having been used for my medicinal benefits and as a charm to repel evil by the ancient Egyptians. My anti-inflammatory properties protect the heart, so take capsules of me daily to assist with any blood pressure and cholesterol concerns and to boost the function of your immune system. To stimulate blood flow and incite arousal eat me raw if you dare, and ingest my pungent aromatic and aphrodisiac powers to invoke a night of stimulated passion!

GARLIC: REPEL

Garlic breath will sure repel
Unwelcome guests, through pungent smell.
Place string of bulbs around your neck
Or over threshold, to protect.
This magick is worked, with harm to none.
So mote it be; there, it is done.

WITCHY RECIPE

This garlic juice is great for improving overall health and fighting the effects of colds and infections. Peel garlic bulbs and use a garlic press to make a garlic purée. Pour the purée into a strainer over a bowl and press down with a rubber spoon to force out the juice. Keep the pulp for flavouring food and store the juice in the fridge.

6 Monday

Mother Shipton (1488-1561), prophetess, soothsayer and witch.

7 Tuesday

8 Wednesday

9 Thursday

Ama Hemmah (1947-2010) was burned to death in Ghana after confessing to being a witch.

10 Friday

11 Saturday

12 Sunday

13 Monday
New moon.

14 Tuesday

15 Wednesday

16 Thursday

17 Friday

18 Saturday

19 Sunday

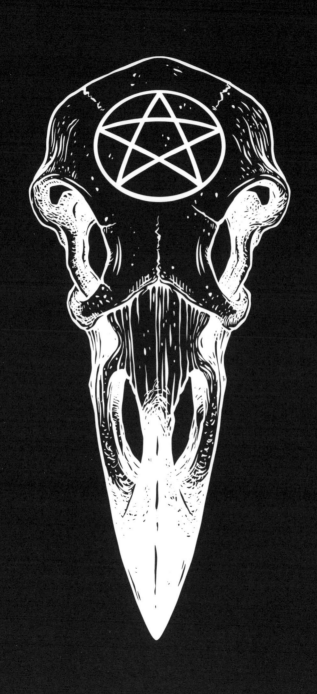

DARK MOON SPELL

Hold a lit black candle under a dark moon and say:

Mistress of mystery, darkness of night
Reveal through the shadows: misery, plight.
Void of all light, black with despair
As darkness consumes me I give up my prayer.
Searching for answers and peace of mind
'Tis me whom I seek, but never to find.
Anguish and fear birthed in cold, dark tomb
Protect me within your deep velvet womb.
Unwelcome company, never alone
I invoke dark moon magick to connect with the crone.

Blow out the candle flame to draw you into the magnetic darkness,
and stay for a while in the protective company of the crone.

20 Monday
First quarter moon.

21 Tuesday

22 Wednesday
Franz Hartmann (1838–1912), occultist, doctor, astrologer and theosophist.

23 Thursday

24 Friday

25 Saturday
Helen Duncan (1897–1956) was the last person imprisoned under the Witchcraft Act of 1735.

26 Sunday

27 Monday
Full moon.

28 Tuesday

29 Wednesday

30 Thursday
Ralph Harvey (1928–2020), occultist, high priest and teacher.

1 Friday
Malleus Maleficarum (Hammer of Witches), which endorsed the extermination of witches, was written by a Catholic clergyman and published in 1487. This book had a strong influence on the witch trials that followed.

2 Saturday
Franz Bardon (1909–58), magician, occultist and teacher of Hermetics.

3 Sunday
More than 123 people were persecuted in India for sorcery and witchcraft between 2016 and 2019.

DECEMBER

Wolf, elder, cold moon

A time of quiet introspection and expectation.

Winter is a mystical artist who paints a breathless picture of landscapes adorned in jewels of sparkling frost and glistening ice. It is a time when your breath is visible on a cold, brisk day, when trees stand stark and bare and nature is stripped to the very core of its former glory. This is a season when mystery hangs in the air as dark nights draw in and envelop the weakened, low-slung sun and when the earth is steeped in deep magick and mystery, which nurtures and restores all that resides within it. It is a time of looking deep within and withdrawing into your inner cave.

December is a month of hardship and discomfort, ensuring trials and tribulations for those ancestors who faced the glacial callousness of winter, for she is a harsh taskmaster and takes no prisoners. It is a time for change, when we acknowledge and honour the cycles of death and rebirth, and a time when hope is renewed. As with the trees of the season we are stripped bare, naked and vulnerable as the macabre presence of the crone shrouds us.

YULE: 21 December

GODDESS: **the Cailleach (Celtic/Scottish)**, the crone who rules over winter begins to fade as the returning sun shines promises of hope, light and a new dawn.

CRONE: hideous queen of winter, bearer of storms, instigator of death.

~ YULE ~

A celebration of the rebirth of the sun, from the darkness growing into the light.

Yule is the sabbat of the winter solstice, the shortest day and the least productive time in nature's annual cycle. This is the longest night, more than 12 hours of darkness as we wait for the dawn. Our ancestors looked forward through the cold barren days of December to the ancient tradition of a midwinter festival.

Yule is a celebration of the rebirth of the sun, for after the longest night the sun will again begin to grow stronger. It is a sacred time of solar rebirth, when we bring into our homes the yule log for the returning sun, mistletoe for fertility and holly for protection. This sabbat represents the rebirth of light. On the longest night of the year the goddess gives birth to the sun god and hope for new light is reborn.

This is a time-honoured tradition when our ancestors and the faeries would gather to welcome the return of the sun, for at the winter solstice the sun is at its weakest, having waned in strength since peaking at the summer solstice, or Litha, six months earlier. Great cheers ring out in celebration, for on the very next winter's morn the sun starts its ascent and steadily becomes stronger as it heads towards the summer months once again. The birth of the sun – the light of the world; the new king is heralded!

This time the oak king prevails over the holly king to bring us the light half of the year. The holly king is the overseer of holly trees, ruling the forests and woods during autumn and winter after battling with the oak king at the summer solstice. They battle again at Yule when the oak king, guardian of oak trees, wins and rules the forests and woods over spring and summer. Their battle reflects the balance of the seasons: the wheel has turned and we celebrate the re-emergence of light out of darkness, bringing renewal of life and the promise of a successful future.

4   Monday

5   Tuesday

Third quarter moon · Pope Innocent VIII published a papal bull condemning witchcraft in 1484.

6   Wednesday

Dion Fortune (1890–1946), occultist and ceremonial magician.

7   Thursday

8   Friday

9   Saturday

10 Sunday

YULE INCANTATION

Faery folk tiptoe soft
Across the land of snow and frost
Towards a holly tree at Yule
'Tis time to cut it from its rule.
For in this battle, oak king wins
To lord over months to take through spring.
And in the morn turn to the sun
Who is born again, the light has won!
Each year the sacred wheel doth turn
Now Yuletide's here, 'tis our concern
To celebrate with joy and mirth
May bells ring out for peace on earth.
So place the logs upon the fire
And make wishes of heart's desire.
Honour the flames that warm the cool
With blessings to one and all this Yule.

WITCH'S WISDOM

Winter requires you to go deep within, to rest and recharge while the protection of the earth nurtures and restores you. Now is the time to connect with the crone aspect of the triple goddess, whose cruel reign over winter leaves the land barren and fruitless, as you journey inwards and face the shadows you have ignored. Allow the frigidness of this harsh month to freeze out any unwanted behaviours, situations or addictions as she strips you bare within the dark chambers of winter's tomb. The colour black represents the element of earth and should be used in accordance with your magickal workings at midnight, when winter rules over the season. In the cycle of life, nature must die before it can rise up and grow again. Your time will come, for death is not the end.

KITCHEN WITCHERY

SUGAR: harness all your desires by adding some sweetness into your life. My sweet crystal power is irreplaceable when it comes to working with sugar magick in ritual and attraction spells. When you utilise my sugary charms I will magnetise all that you wish to allure, such as a lover, friendship, money and beauty, as you cast candy spells. Sprinkle me in nature to summon the elementals or burn a cube to communicate with the spirits you wish to invoke. As I sweeten any culinary dish I'll delight you on the tongue and entice your taste buds. When your mood turns sour, burn me to sweeten you up or perform some sweetening magick on another whose words have a bitter edge. As you sugar-coat a situation you are supported by the sweet smell of magick, which really will be the icing on the cake.

INCANTATION

Winter's hard, but you'll survive
As crone strips you while still alive.
This season's magick is laid bare.
New wisdom's found within to share.
This magick is worked, with harm to none.
So mote it be; there, it is done.

SUGAR: SWEETNESS

Desserts, candies are a weakness
Inviting in a little sweetness.
Sprinkle, pour, mix in well
Attract desires with sugar spell.
This magick is worked with harm to none.
So mote it be; there, it is done.

DECEMBER

11 Monday

12 Tuesday
New moon.

13 Wednesday

14 Thursday

15 Friday
Anna Franklin (1955-), high priestess and bestselling author of more than 20 books on witchcraft · Amina Bint Abdul Halim bin Salem Nasser beheaded in Saudi Arabia in 2011 for practising witchcraft.

16 Saturday
In Tanzania more than 40,000 people have been accused of witchcraft; many were tried and killed between 1960 and 2000.

17 Sunday

18   Monday

Edith Rose Woodford-Grimes (1887–1975), one of the first adherents of English wicca and the working partner of Gerald Gardner.

19   Tuesday

First quarter moon · Ronald Hutton (1953-), historian specialising in witchcraft, paganism and British folklore.

20   Wednesday

21   Thursday

Yule, winter solstice, midwinter.

22   Friday

23   Saturday

24   Sunday

WITCHY RECIPE

This scrub is great for the face, body, feet and hands. Mix 1 cup of white or brown organic sugar with ½ cup of sunflower oil or another carrier oil such as coconut in a mixing bowl. Add essential oils of your choice such as lemon, lavender or cumin. Add Himalayan salt for a courser scrub. Mix together and store in a Mason jar.

WITCHY TIP

An original tradition is to bring evergreen trees and sprigs into the household for protection and to honour the wood spirits by offering them a place to keep warm during the fragile, cold months of winter. Use sprigs of rosemary, sage, thyme, basil and mint to make a special wreath, which will invite goodwill and cheer to your table. Pine cones symbolise enlightenment and make great place-setting holders. Cinnamon sticks and holly berries in the home symbolise protection, and a dried orange slice symbolises good fortune.

WISH TREE SPELL

Once you've decorated your home in true witchy Yule style, write your wishes on glittery pieces of paper, material or ribbons and say:

From this wreath I carefully choose
A herb or two, I need to use.
For flavour gives the food a lift
With thanks I consume nature's gift.
A magick space we doth create
Tree is chosen, 'tis its fate!
Holly doth protect me well
Orange slice for fortune spell.
Pretty pine cones place you here
To bring us all hope, joy and cheer.
Let's celebrate with songs and mirth
May bells ring out for peace on earth.
Welcome spirits, every one
Let's celebrate return of sun!
Magick abounds, my wish is done.
May it come true, with harm none.

Tie your wishes to the tree
so they can come true.

25 Monday

26 Tuesday

27 Wednesday
Full moon.

28 Thursday

29 Friday

30 Saturday
Maxine Sanders (1946–), high priestess and occultist.

31 Sunday

WITCHES OF ROYALTY

JOAN OF NAVARRE, *Queen of England*
Born: c.1368 | **Died:** 10 June 1437
Accused of witchcraft

ELEANOR COBHAM, *Duchess of Gloucester*
Born: c.1400 | **Died:** 7 July 1452
Accused of witchcraft

JACQUETTA WOODVILLE, *Duchess of Bedford*
Born: c.1416 | **Died:** 30 May 1472
Accused of witchcraft

ELIZABETH WOODVILLE, *Queen of England*
Born: c.1437 | **Died:** 8 June 1492
Accused of witchcraft

Witches' museums, memorials and places to visit

Arnemetia's Mystical Emporium, Buxton, UK
Mother Shipton's Cave, Knaresborough, UK
Museum of Witchcraft and Magic, Boscastle, Cornwall, UK
Pendle Heritage Centre, Barrowford, Lancaster, UK
Museum of Witchcraft and Wizardry, Stratford on Avon, UK
Salem Witch Museum and Memorial, Salem, Massachusetts, USA
Buckland Museum of Witchcraft and Magick, Cleveland, Ohio, USA
New Orleans Historic Voodoo Museum, New Orleans, Louisiana, USA
Museum of Icelandic Sorcery and Witchcraft, Hólmavík, Iceland
Witches Weigh House, Oudewater, Netherlands
Magicum – Berlin Magic Museum, Berlin, Germany
Hexenmuseum Schweiz, Gränichen, Switzerland
Witches Museum, Zugarramurdi, Spain

Witch organisations

Children of Artemis
Witchcraft.org

UK Pagan Federation
Paganfed.org